Improving Services for Young Children

From Sure Start to Children's Centres

Improving Services for Young Children

From Sure Start to Children's Centres

Edited by
Angela Anning and Mog Ball

Los Angeles • London • New Delhi • Singapore

SAGE Publications Ltd
1 Oliver's Yard
55 City Road
London EC1Y 1SP

SAGE Publications Inc.
2455 Teller Road
Thousand Oaks, California 91320

SAGE Publications India Pvt Ltd
B 1/I 1 Mohan Cooperative Industrial Area
Mathura Road
New Delhi 110 044

SAGE Publications Asia-Pacific Pte Ltd
33 Pekin Street #02-01
Far East Square
Singapore 048763

Library of Congress Control Number: 2007940393

British Library Cataloguing in Publication data

A catalogue record for this book is available from the British Library

ISBN 978-1-4129-4821-0
ISBN 978-1-4129-4822-7 (pbk)

Typeset by C&M Digitals (P) Ltd., Chennai, India
Printed in India at Replika Press Pvt Ltd
Printed on paper from sustainable resources

Contents

List of Figures and Tables

Figure

Tables

List of Contributors

Angela Jane Edwards Anning Emeritus Professor of Early Childhood Education, University of Leeds and Principal Investigator for NESS (National Evaluation of Sure Start), Birkbeck College, London. Angela has experience in the field as early years teacher and as headteacher in inner city primary schools. She is a trainer of early years teachers and professionals delivering children's services, and a researcher into professional knowledge applied to practice in integrated service settings. Her recent relevant publications include: Anning and Edwards, *Promoting Children's Learning from Birth to Five: Developing the New Early Years Professional* (2nd edition, 2006, Open University Press); Anning, Cullen and Fleer (eds), *Early Childhood Education: Society and Culture* (2004, 2nd edition in press, Sage); Anning et al. *Developing Multi-professional Teamwork for Integrated Children's Services* (2006, Open University Press).

Mog Ball Honorary Associate Research Fellow and Principal Investigator for NESS, Institute for the Study of Children, Families and Social Issues, Birkbeck, University of London. Mog is a writer and researcher on a wide range of social programmes. Her publications include: *Evaluation in the Voluntary Sector* (1986, Home Office); *Domestic Violence and Social Care* (1996, Department of Health); *School Inclusion: The School, the Family, the Community* (1998, Joseph Rowntree Foundation); *Understanding Parents' Needs* (2001, National Family and Parenting Institute); *Intervening Early* (2002, DfES and Coram Family). She also drafted *The Practice Guide for Children's Centres* published by the DfES in November 2005.

Jane Barlow Professor in Public Health, Warwick Medical School, University of Warwick. Jane is a researcher evaluating the effectiveness of early interventions in the primary prevention of mental health problems. Her publications include: *Family and Parent Support in Sure Start* (2006, DfES); *Learning from the Family Support Grant* (2005, DfES); *The Clinical and Cost-effectiveness of Different Parent Training Programmes for Children with Behaviour Problems: A Systematic Review and Economic Evaluation* (2006, NICE); *The Effectiveness of Parenting Programmes for Ethnic Minority Parents* (2004, Joseph Rowntree Foundation).

Gary Craig   Professor of Social Justice, Head of the Centre for Social Inclusion and Social Justice, and Associate Director at the Wilberforce Institute for the Study of Slavery and Emancipation at the University of Hull. Gary's main research interests include poverty and deprivation, local governance, children and young people, community development and 'race' and ethnicity. He led the National Evaluation of the Local Network Fund (DfES), the review of the experience of the Children's Fund for the Children's Society, and many studies of 'race' and welfare. He has also been a social policy consultant to Family Services Units, Children's Society and Barnardos. His recent publications include: *The Local Network Fund, The National Evaluation* (2005, DfES); *Living on the Edge* (teenage pregnancy in rural areas) (2004, DoH); *Community Development with Children* (2000, Barnardos); *The Children's Fund?* (2005, Children's Society); 'Black and minority ethnic children' (in *At Greatest Risk?* G. Preston, ed., 2005, Child Poverty Action Group).

Sir David Hall   Emeritus Professor of Community Paediatrics, University of Sheffield, member of the NESS team. Sir David's report *Health for All Children* (1989, Oxford University Press) influenced thinking on preventative services for children in countries all over the world. He was President of the Royal College of Paediatrics and Child Health from 2000 to 2003, and has published over 100 papers, three books (in several editions) and 11 book chapters. Recently he edited, with Professor Lewis Leavitt, *Social and Moral Development: Emerging Evidence on the Toddler Years* (2002, Johnson and Johnson Paediatric Institute).

Sue Kirkpatrick   Associate Research Fellow at University of Warwick and independent research consultant, specialising in qualitative research about children and families. Sue's work focuses primarily on issues relating to social exclusion and parenting.

Jenny McLeish   Strategic Co-ordinator of the National Teenage Pregnancy Midwifery Network, and researcher, writer and campaigner on marginalised women's access to maternity services. Jenny's publications include: *Talking about Food: How to Give Effective Healthy Eating Advice to Disadvantaged Pregnant Women* (2005, Maternity Alliance); *Challenges Midwives Face when Caring for Asylum Seekers* (in *Challenges for Midwives* Volume 1, Richens, ed., 2005, Quay Books); *Mothers in Exile: Maternity Experiences of Asylum Seekers and their Babies* (2002, Maternity Alliance); *A Crying Shame: Pregnant Asylum Seekers and their Babies in Detention* (2002, Maternity Alliance).

Pamela Meadows   Visiting Fellow at the National Institute of Economic and Social Research. Pamela is Director of the cost-effectiveness module of the National Evaluation of Sure Start and is also currently evaluating the outcomes and cost-effectiveness of literacy and numeracy training for adults. She recently provided consultancy advice to the consortium led by the University of New South Wales in Sydney, on the design of the cost-effectiveness evaluation of the federal government's *Stronger Families and Communities Programme* in Australia. She is currently working with the University of New South Wales on the cost-effectiveness evaluation of the New South Wales government's Early Intervention Programme. In the past Pamela has examined the cost-effectiveness of the Assessment Framework for children in need, funded by the Department of Health. Her previous research included two studies of childcare: one of workforce recruitment and retention in childcare, and the second looking at the geographical area within which parents look for childcare. She was formerly Director of the Policy Studies Institute, and before that was Chief Economist and Head of Economics Research and Evaluation at the Department of Employment.

Lisa Niven   Research Officer at the Institute for the Study of Children, Families and Social Issues, Birkbeck, University of London. Lisa has an MA in Education (Psychology) from the Institute of Education, University of London. Her publications include: Ball and Niven *Buildings in Sure Start Local Programmes* (2005, DfES); Ball et al.

Outreach and Home Visiting Services in Sure Start Local Programmes (2007, DfES).

Caroline Pickstone   Speech & Language Therapist, service manager and clinical research fellow, School for Health & Related Research, University of Sheffield. Caroline has worked on the development of integrated working models for children's services through early involvement with trailblazer Sure Start programmes, subsequently offering consultancy advice to programmes to assist their development of services. She has carried out doctoral research work on early language development and is particularly interested in issues of accessibility and use of services. She is a co-editor of *Learning from Sure Start* (2005, Open University Press), which details the findings and impact of one local Sure Start Trailblazer programme.

Veronica Sawyer   Research Officer, Institute for the Study of Children, Families and Social Issues, Birkbeck, University of London. Veronica is an experienced primary school teacher and curriculum manager, as well as a trainer of primary and early years teachers. Her PhD concerned the training and professional knowledge of primary and early years teachers in university–school partnership settings, and she has carried out research in primary, early years and nursery settings.

Sarah Stewart-Brown   Professor of Public Health at Warwick Medical School. Sarah worked in the UK National Health Service from 1975 onwards, first as a paediatrician and subsequently as a public health doctor in London, Bristol and Worcester. She has also held academic appointments at the Departments of Child Health and of Epidemiology and Community Health at the University of Bristol. Before joining Warwick Medical School she was a Reader in the Department of Public Health at the University of Oxford where she directed the Health Services Research Unit. Sarah's research covers many aspects of public health, but her special interest areas are child public health and health promotion. Her current research interests include emotional and social development and its contribution to the mental and physical health of both adults and children.

Fiona Williams   Professor of Social Policy in the School of Sociology and Social Policy at the University of Leeds, and Director of the CAVA Research Centre at Leeds University. Fiona has published widely in social policy. Her books include: *Social Policy: A Critical Introduction. Issues of Race, Gender and Class* (1989, Polity Press); *Welfare Research: A Critical Review* (with J. Popay and A. Oakley, 1999; *Rethinking Families* (2004, Calouste Gulbenkian Foundation); *Gendering Citizenship in Western Europe* (co-authored with A. Antonnen et al., 2007, The Policy Press); and *Empowering Parents in Local Sure Start Programmes* (with H. Churchill, 2007, DfES). Her current research is on the increasing employment of migrant workers as home-based child carers.

Glossary

Children's Centres   Centres were set up from 2005. They are administered by the children's services arm of local authorities. They provide multi-agency services intended to be flexible in meeting the needs of families with children from birth to school age. Core offers include integrated early education, childcare, family support, health services, outreach and employment advice. Many centres will share sites with schools. In the long term there will be one Sure Start Children's Centre for every community, promised by 2010.

Children's Trusts   Trusts are bodies responsible for the joint commissioning of local children's services and for overseeing the pooled resources of agencies such as education, social services and health.

Community development   A process of working with people, usually those living with some disadvantage, to enable them to improve their situation through their own efforts in ways which suit them and meet their aspirations. Community workers are trained in supporting this process, which is essentially one of empowering people.

Early Years Professionals   By 2010 all Sure Start Children's Centres will employ a new Early Years Professional (EYP) to plan and lead the delivery of integrated day care and early learning provision. The Children's Workforce Council has outlined the qualifications for this new professional. It is anticipated that many of them will be qualified teachers who have undertaken additional training to achieve EYP status.

Empowerment   A shift from a state of vulnerability or lack of power to enhanced power or control. Empowerment can be at individual, group or community levels.

ESOL   English for Speakers of Other Languages.

Extended schools By 2010 networks of local schools will ensure that all school-aged children and their parents are able to access a core offer of services. These include homework clubs, recreational activities, high-quality childcare between the hours of 8 a.m. and 6 p.m. all year round, parenting support programmes and access to specialist services such as speech and language therapy and intensive behaviour support. Extended schools will also offer adult learning and recreational facilities to the wider community.

Every Child Matters The government policy document which resulted in the Children Act 2004. Five broad outcomes for children were defined: being healthy, being protected from harm and neglect, being enabled to enjoy and achieve, making a positive contribution to society and contributing to economic well-being.

Intermediate labour market A scheme for providing those who are most removed from the labour market with a bridge back to the world of work by providing paid work on a temporary contract together with training, personal development and job search support.

Learning and Skills Council (LSC) The body responsible for planning and funding education and training for people over the age of 16 in England.

National Evaluation of Sure Start (NESS) The largest evaluation of a social programme ever commissioned by the British government, this study began in 2001 measuring the impact of 250 local programmes on various indicators of child and parent functions. Elements of the study also looked at the working of the programmes, their local context and their cost effectiveness. The longitudinal study which is part of the evaluation is likely to continue collecting data for some time.

New Deal for Communities (NDC) A key part of the government's strategy to combat multiple deprivation in deprived neighbourhoods. The 39 NDC projects aim to tackle worklessness, crime, education, health and housing and the physical environment.

National Vocational Qualification (NVQ) NVQs cover five levels from Level 1, which covers competence in routine and predictable work, to Level 5, which requires competence in the application of a range of fundamental principles across a wide and often unpredictable variety of contexts.

National Service Framework (NSF) Department of Health and Department for Education and Skills (2004) *National Service Framework for Children, Young People and Maternity Services*. London: Department of Health. (Available at www.dh.gov.uk/

Policy AndGuidance/HealthAndSocialCareTopics/ChildrenServices/Children ServicesInformation/fs/en). In response to the recommendations in the Kennedy Report, a National Service Framework (NSF) was commissioned in 2001 and published in 2004. The NSF was probably the most comprehensive exposition of child health policy undertaken anywhere in the world and took a very broad view of what is meant by health. Among many recommendations it endorsed previous policy developments in the fields of early detection, child mental health and child protection and reinforced guidance on inter-disciplinary collaboration. Many of the concepts enshrined in the Sure Start programme were incorporated in the policy proposals.

Neighbourhood nurseries   Daycare facilities introduced in 2001, using public/private finance initiatives (that is, costs shared between statutory and private sector interests), to narrow the gap in high-quality, accessible full day childcare provision for children up to the age of five in the most disadvantaged areas of England. The aim was to encourage parents to work or to attend training leading to work.

Professionals   Workers who have been qualified and trained according to a recognised standard accredited by professional body. **Professional practices** are the bureaucratic and formal aspects of the way professionals work, underpinned by their values and beliefs in the causes of and solutions for problems. **Practitioners** are also qualified and trained workers, but they will not be members of such long-established regulatory bodies.

Safeguarding children   The process, shared across agencies, of protecting children from neglect and abuse, preventing impairment of their health and development, and ensuring that they grow up in circumstances consistent with the provision of safe and effective care, which is undertaken so as to enable children to have optimum life chances and enter adulthood successfully.

Sure Start Local Programmes (SSLPs)   Programmes set up in areas defined as the most disadvantaged in England from 1998, until there were over 500 by 2004. Wales, Scotland and Northern Ireland developed parallel Sure Start plans. The programmes were locally administered by partnerships between statutory agencies (such as local authorities and primary care trusts) and the voluntary and private sector. Their remit was to join up services, using multi-agency teams, to deliver core programmes in innovative or improved ways for child and maternal health, early education and play, childcare, family support and employment/training opportunities for all families in the area with children under the age of four. There was an emphasis on outreach/home visiting to provide access for 'hard-to-reach' families.

The Early Years Foundation Stage   From September 2008, all settings offering early years provision are required to deliver a single, coherent framework of integrated care and early education.

The Laming Report   The report was an inquiry into the death of Victoria Climbié (HMSO, 2003). Lord Laming chaired an enquiry into the torture and murder of Victoria Climbié. His report reviewed the sequential failures in the child protection system and emphasised the importance of inter-agency collaboration and training. The Government acknowledged the need to safeguard children more effectively and the proposals were incorporated in a series of papers under the overall title *Every Child Matters*.

The Report of the Public Inquiry into Children's Heart Surgery at the Bristol Royal Infirmary 1984–95: *Learning from Bristol* (Cm 5207), (HMSO, 2001). Following public concern about the quality of children's heart surgery in Bristol, a comprehensive review of children's health care was undertaken by Professor Ian Kennedy. Professor Kennedy criticised 'in some anger' the neglect of children's services by successive governments. The Department of Health's response was published in 2002 by The Stationery Office.

United Nations Convention on the Rights of the Child   Implemented by the UK government since 1992, it lists 40 distinctive rights covering safety, health, education and happiness and the significant 'Right to be heard' contained in Article 12. This has led to a new emphasis on listening to the opinions and wishes of even the youngest children.

Introduction

Readers of this book will be interested in working in, or planning to work in, the developing field of services for children and their families. Their concerns are likely to be the knowledge and skills required by the children's services workforce. In the book we try to address both knowledge and skills. The first involves a broad, inter-disciplinary understanding of how children develop and families work in the context of their communities. The second is about learning how to do things to improve the life chances for children through good-quality professional practice.

The book draws on real-life experiences gained through the Sure Start intervention. Sure Start local programmes offered an opportunity for practitioners to learn from each other, and this happened at several levels. They were able to learn from colleagues within multi-disciplinary teams, from practitioners from other agencies and organisations, and from the families and communities with whom they were working.

Sure Start has offered a model of a learning community. It had a deeply serious moral purpose in addressing poverty and social exclusion. It was backed by a large-scale financial commitment from central government, and through the mechanism of local decision-making it provided flexibility to explore new ways of working. Although this left Sure Start open to the criticism that the intervention was loose and unstructured, it enabled communities to conduct serious experiments in the improvement of services for families.

Here we share what we have learned from the Sure Start experience where it is relevant for the development of the children's service workforce. The contribution to the knowledge base includes child development, child welfare and helping children progress. The acquisition of skills includes those of effective communication and engagement, sharing information, and multi-agency teamwork. Overarching themes have emerged: the ethics of social engineering and intervening in children's lives; the complexity of maintaining quality while promoting innovation; establishing respectful relationships between practitioners and users; the deployment of generic and specialist skills; and how to design services that reach everybody. The chapters of the book are grouped under headings which reflect these themes.

1 What was Sure Start and Why Did it Matter?

Angela Anning and David Hall

Sure Start

Sure Start was a £500 million anti-poverty intervention set up in the UK in 1998 and funded by the New Labour Government Treasury Department under the leadership of the then Chancellor, Gordon Brown. It was designed as a 10-year programme, targeting all the families with children under four years old living in more than 500 of the most disadvantaged communities.

But Sure Start did not come 'out of the blue'. Its story is part of a series of policy changes in children's services; and the design of Sure Start drew on a history of international research evidence on the effectiveness of early interventions to improve the health, well-being and educational attainments of disadvantaged children.

We outline the history of policy and research in services for young children over the last two decades (1997–2007), before returning to the place of the Sure Start model within this history and to the evaluation of Sure Start Local Programmes (SSLPs), which is the focus of this book.

Policy

In 1997 when New Labour came to power, the modernisation of public services was high on their agenda. Tony Blair (1998) proclaimed four key principles:

1   High standards and full accountability.
2   Devolution of decision-making about service delivery to the 'front line'.
3   Flexibility of employment.
4   Involving the voluntary and private sector to increase choice for users.

The first principle of accountability, high standards and (by implication) best value for money implied government control, with inspections and measurements against centrally prescribed targets. This imperative sits uneasily with the other three principles: devolution of decision-making from central to local control, flexibility of employment for workers, and increasing the stakeholders involved in delivering services and therefore offering more choice to parents. These three should promote the genuine empowerment of providers and users of services in local communities. The story of Sure Start exemplified the tension between the rhetoric of local empowerment and the realities of central government control.

From the start, the Brown–Blair partnership acknowledged the interconnectedness of economic and social reforms. Critiques of the old-style public sector monoliths generated arguments for 'joined-up thinking' in the fields of health, education, childcare, social services, law enforcement, housing, employment and family support. The government's aim was to reshape services: to make them more flexible and responsive to local demographics and priorities, more efficient by reducing overlap in diagnoses, treatments and record-keeping, and ultimately more effective. The history of Sure Start Local Programmes (from 1998 to 2004) was intertwined with these broader policy initiatives in the UK.

Two Green Papers, *Every Child Matters* (DfES, 2003) and *Every Child Matters: Change for Children* (DfES, 2004) (www.everychildmatters.gov.uk/multiagencyworking) led to the Children Act of 2004. Five broad outcomes were defined for all children from birth to 18: being healthy; being protected from harm and neglect; being enabled to enjoy and achieve; making a positive contribution to society; and contributing to economic well-being. The intention was that services should work together to respond to the needs of the whole child *and* their family. The Sure Start Unit was set up to co-ordinate all departments responsible for services for young children, including the Departments of Health (DoH), which had responsibility for social services, and Education and Skills (DfES). Later the Unit was absorbed into the DfES. In 2003 the first Minister for Children, Young People and Families was appointed. Regional centres staffed by civil servants were set up, with directors responsible for promoting the infrastructures to enable 'joined-up working' to happen. In March 2006 all Local Authorities were charged with employing a director to co-ordinate children's services. This was in response to high-profile failures to protect young children from neglect and harm, such as the Victoria Climbié case referenced later in the chapter. Children's Trusts, bodies responsible for joint commissioning of local children's services and pooled resources across agencies were to be in place by 2008. The infrastructure of Trusts was underpinned by five principles: child-centred, outcome-led vision; integrated front-line delivery of services; integrated processes; joint planning and commissioning strategies; and inter-agency governance. Trusts were required to demonstrate effective leadership at every level, including front-line delivery, performance management driving an outcomes focus (from area inspections to rewards and incentives for individual staff), and strategies to listen to children and young people.

Whilst the roller coaster of reforms *across* the agencies delivering children's services swept along, individual agencies were having to respond to policy changes. In Health, a *National Service Framework for Children, Young People and Maternity Services* (DfES/DoH, 2004) and the White Paper, *Choosing Health* (DoH, 2004) (www.dh.gov.uk) emphasised the importance of medical workers collaborating with social workers, nursing staff and other agencies to plan and deliver services, including information-sharing, to children within locally defined communities. Health agencies had specific targets: for example, percentage of 4–5-year-olds who were obese and percentage of mothers initiating breast-feeding.

In Education, since April 2004, all 3- and 4-year-olds have been entitled to a free, good-quality, part-time early education place (currently 12.5 hours per week for 38 weeks of the year). Parents can choose to access free places from a range of early education provision in the maintained, voluntary or private sectors. All providers, including childminders, must deliver the *Birth to Three Matters* curriculum (DfES, 2002) for 0–3-year-olds and *Foundation Stage* (DfEE/QCA, 2000) for 3–5-year-olds (www.standards.dfes.gov.uk/primary/publications.foundation_stage). From 2008 these two curricula combined into a single, coherent framework, the *Early Years Foundation Stage*, for the delivery of education and care. Under the duties of the Childcare Act 2006, practitioners were required to complete an Early Years Foundation Stage profile for each child. The profile records a child's progression in physical, intellectual, emotional and social development against 13 assessment scales. By the time they start compulsory schooling at five, children are expected to score 78 points, with at least six points in the personal/social/emotional and communication/language/literacy scales. Local authorities return data, at individual child level, to the Department for Children, Families and Schools (DCFS). As progression will be traceable to the services/settings the child used, this level of accountability could be taxing for early years settings.

In childcare, a Green Paper, *Meeting the Childcare Challenge* (DfEE, 1998), set a target for developing 100,000 new childcare places for 2008. A *Ten Year Strategy for Childcare* (DfES, 2005a) predicted out-of-school childcare places for all 3–14-year-olds from 8a.m. to 6p.m. every weekday by 2010. There is increasing economic pressure on families for both parents to work and targets for local authorities to reduce the percentage of households dependent on workless benefits and to increase the percentage of teenage mothers in education, employment or training. Neighbourhood nursery initiatives, providing day care for under-fives to release parents to return to work, were funded by public/private initiatives (PFIs), often in former SSLP neighbourhoods. The expansion of childcare was linked to an ambitious agenda towards extended schools. Primary and secondary and special schools are expected to serve as a hub for services for families with school-aged children. As well as before- and after-school care, schools are expected to franchise activities such as sport, drama, dance, homework clubs, IT facilities and training, parenting and family support. They co-ordinate referrals for specialist treatments from, for example, speech and language therapists or mental health workers. By 2010, 3,500 Sure Start children's centres will be established in communities to serve as the hub of a similar range of services for families with pre-school-age children.

Finally, in Social Services the tragic case of Victoria Climbié, who was tortured and murdered in 2000 whilst supposedly being monitored by health, social services and police workers, triggered a government enquiry culminating in the *Laming Report* (Laming, 2003). Laming was highly critical of local authority departments' inability to work together, and recommended that there should be a Directorate of Children's Services in each local authority. The term 'safeguarding' replaced 'child protection' to emphasise the message that it was the responsibility of *all* professionals working with children to promote their health and development. A common assessment framework (CAF) is the standardised tool for assessing the needs of children for services (www.everychildmatters.gov.uk/deliveringservices/caf). It can be used on its own or with specialist or universal assessment tools. It consists of a pre-assessment checklist to identify if a child needs a CAF; a protocol for collecting the views of the child, parent/carers and relevant professionals on the strengths and needs of the child; and a pro forma for recording and, where appropriate, sharing information across agencies about the assessments and treatments. A key professional, possibly the child's teacher or social worker, will manage each case.

The implementation of this raft of radical changes in children's services was monitored by a complex inspection system. The centrally-imposed systems of accountability implied a distrust of professionals doing their jobs properly. It is another example of the rhetoric of empowerment of practitioners being undermined by the realities of micro-management from central government control. Alongside centrally-imposed government inspections, individual settings were required to operate regular, detailed and time-consuming self-evaluation schemes. Now local authority children's services have Joint Area Reviews, concurrent with auditing from the Audit Commission. Inspection teams include representation from the Office for Standards in Education (Ofsted), Commission for Social Care Inspection (CSCI), Health Care Commission (HCC) and Adult Learning Inspection (ALI). Local authorities have to demonstrate that they have surveyed the views of 600 representative children and young people using a web-based 'Tellus' questionnaire survey. The ponderous industry of accountability is thriving. Professionals have felt disempowered, with their autonomy threatened by its bureaucratic demands.

The government initiated a children's workforce reform strategy to prepare staff for new ways of working. A Children's Workforce Development Council (CWDC) (www.cwdcouncil.org.uk) is responsible for upgrading the workforce. Since we know that in 2006 more than half the personnel in care services were not qualified beyond Level 2 (the equivalent of a diploma), this is an uphill task. In contrast, in schools 80 per cent of those working with under-fives were qualified at Level 4 (degree level). Social work training was reformed towards graduate and registered status, with bursaries provided for social work students (www.gscc.org.uk).

But there are still lively debates about how to retain specialisms in training, such as teachers (who remain isolated from the CWDC reforms within the Teacher Development Agency remit) or health visitors, trained within healthcare systems, while ensuring that all early years workers share common core skills and knowledge (DfES, 2005b). A new concept of an Early Years Professional (EYP) developed, a pedagogue of graduate status trained to work across the sectors of care, learning and health. There will be an EYP in all Sure Start children's centres by 2010, in day-care settings by 2015 and in the long term in every foundation stage setting. The blurring of the distinction between a teacher and an EYP raises the possibility of a distinct (and perhaps lower paid/lower status) category of teachers trained for pre-school settings.

The government also recognised the complexity of managing change within the structural systems of services for young children (Aubrey, 2007). All managers of children's centres are now required to have a graduate status National Professional Qualification in Integrated Centre Leadership (NPQICL), managed by the National College of School Leadership (www.ncsl.org.uk/programmes/npqicl/index.cfm).

Research

The government claimed that its public service reforms were 'evidence-based'. It commissioned reviews of research evidence in key policy areas (for example, of the impact of early years provision on young children [Melhuish, 2004] and what works in parenting support [Morgan et al., 2004]. But research findings in the social sciences are often irritatingly contradictory and ambivalent. Policy-makers can cherry-pick reports for evidence to justify their preferred course of action. However, before Sure Start Local Programmes were set up in 1998 a great deal of care was taken to review relevant research in the field and to apply findings to the design of the intervention (Utting, 1999).

The government also commissioned expensive evaluations of initiatives such as Children's Trusts (www.everychildmatters.gov.uk/childrenstrusts) and indeed the Sure Start intervention (www.ness.bbk.uk). But the problem with large-scale evaluations of government programmes is that they are bedevilled by the complexity of what they are expected to deliver. Governments want quick evidence of 'what works'. In reality, evaluations often become redundant before their end dates, as so-called pilot phases are rolled out, albeit modified, in line with political and economic imperatives (Bilson, 2005). However, it was the belief that information from evaluations funded by taxpayers should be widely disseminated that drove the publication of this book. As Young et al. argued: 'Research can serve the public good just as effectively when it seeks to enlighten and inform in the interests of generating wider public debate. Not evidence-based policy, but a broader evidence-informed society is the appropriate aim' (2002: 223).

The architect of the Sure Start intervention was the economist Norman Glass (1999). He based his argument for Sure Start on evidence from the USA (Shonkoff and Meisels, 2000). Randomised controlled trials of early interventions demonstrated benefits for disadvantaged children of high-quality pre-school provision from birth to 5-years-old. Examples cited were the Abecedarian Project (Ramey and Campbell, 1991) and the Perry Pre-school Project (Schweinhart et al., 1993). Small-scale, tightly controlled interventions produced evidence of larger effects on the children than more ambitious large-scale interventions. Yet large-scale US interventions, such as the Chicago Parent–Child Centers (Reynolds et al., 2001) and Headstart (Karoly et al., 1998), often combining centre-based with home-based services, did show benefits. There was also evidence that home visiting by nurse-qualified staff, rather than by para-professionals, particularly if their approach to treatments was highly structured, benefited families (Olds et al., 2004a, 2004b). The overall message from research was that money spent on early preventative interventions was likely to save money on remedial services for children later in life; *but* that only sustained, high-quality interventions were effective (Melhuish, 2004; Olds, 2002).

Evidence accumulated of the inter-relationships between unemployment, poverty, crime, child abuse and neglect, substance abuse and parental mental health and poor child outcomes. Yet attempts to 'regenerate' communities defined as living in poverty, often funded for limited periods under a succession of banners, had limited success. Built into the Sure Start initiative was the concept of community involvement in decision-making, management and delivery of services, exemplified in this statement: 'Public services should be user not provider driven, evidence based, joined up and innovative' (Melhuish and Hall, 2007). There was limited research evidence to support the principles, but they were consistent with New Labour's approach to reform.

In health, two key constructs informed the design of early childhood interventions (Shonkoff and Phillips, 2000). The concept of 'critical periods' in child development stimulated programmes to screen young children for disorders so that appropriate treatments (such as speech and language therapy or physiotherapy) were applied as soon as possible. In parallel, there was interest in 'brain plasticity' – the idea that the infant brain developed rapidly and had a great capacity for new learning. However, 'developmental screening' was problematic. This was partly because there are wide variations in 'normal' development in language and motor skills, often making diagnosis of conditions difficult in very young children (Bishop, 2000). Children with major disorders tended to self-refer via parents and their general practitioners (GPs), rather than as a result of expensive screening programmes. But diagnoses of minor disorders, such as dyslexia and attention deficit hyperactivity disorder (ADHD), were often missed, and were over-represented in lower social classes. In the UK the emphasis shifted from developmental screening to preventative, health-promotion strategies (Blair and Hall, 2006). There was disquiet amongst some paediatricians about the change in policy, but it was welcomed by school nurses and health visitors.

Research evidence of the effectiveness of multi-agency teamwork in delivering services was also scarce, though there had been enquiries into their processes. Examples in the UK were Cameron and Lart (2003), Tomlinson (2003), Sloper (2004) and Anning et al. (2006). Evidence was of recurring dilemmas in translating the policy of joined-up working into practice. Problems included: reconciling different professional beliefs and practices; managing staff on different pay scales and with different conditions of service; combining funding streams from single agency infrastructures; and a lack of joint training and opportunities for professional development for both leaders and led in multi-agency teams. In the field of safeguarding children, Hallett and Birchall (1992) concluded that there was no clear evidence of better protection in multi-agency approaches for vulnerable or excluded children. And in a study in the USA, Glisson and Hemmelgarn (1998) argued that improving positive organisational climates within services was more beneficial in terms of outcomes for children than diverting professionals' attention to working across professional boundaries. The jury seems to be out on the impact on providers of multi-agency teamwork, and it is early days to measure its impact on users.

The birth of Sure Start

There was increasing concern about the cumulative effects of social exclusion on children's trajectories and life chances at international level (with interventions in Canada and Australia as well in the UK and USA). Influential reports pre-dating Sure Start were published by the Luxembourg Income Study (www.lisproject.org). The Labour government commissioned a series of inter-departmental seminars in 1998 which generated ideas for anti-poverty initiatives, including Sure Start, and A Guide to Evidence Based Practice was published in 1999 (Utting 1999). But the level of child poverty in the UK remains high by

European standards and the gap between rich and poor is growing. Between 22 and 48 months, the attainments and health of children with the same cognitive and physical developmental measures, but from different socio-economic backgrounds, begin to drift apart. By the age of six, the differential trends are set towards adulthood. Sure Start was a radical and courageous attempt to lift some of the most vulnerable children in the UK out of cycles of educational under-achievement, poor health, limited employment opportunities and low aspirations.

The underpinning theoretical model was Bronfenbrenner's (1979) ecological model of child development. He argued for the importance of 'the recognition that environmental events and conditions outside any immediate setting containing the person can have a profound influence on behaviour and development within that setting' (1979: 18). He emphasised the active role people play in shaping their environment, 'a growing, dynamic entity that progressively moves into and restructures the milieu in which it resides' (1979: 21). He believed that 'the interaction between a person and an environment is viewed as two-dimensional, that is characterised by reciprocity' (1979: 22). His model, set out in Figure 1.1, defines a complex hierarchy of systems in which the actions of people are nested.

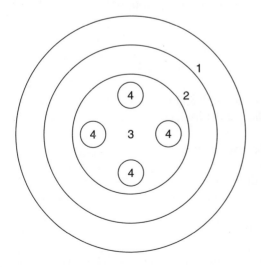

4 Micro-system: for example, the playgroup, pre-school education, childcare or childminder setting where the child actively experiences a particular pattern of events, roles and interpersonal relationships.

3 Meso-system: interrelations between two or more settings in which the child actively participates – for example, home and nursery, childminder and playgroup.

2 Exo-system: settings that do not involve the child as an active participant but in which events occur that affect, or are affected by, what happens in the micro-systems – for example, local authority systems or inspection structures.

1 Macro-system: historical/social/cultural/ecological environments at national policy level.

Figure 1.1   Historical/cultural influences on services for the developing child (based on Bronfenbrenner, 1979)

The Sure Start intervention took this holistic approach to raising the life-chances of young children, nested in families, in turn nested in whole communities as its starting point. It was a universal area-based intervention targeting very deprived areas with the aim of lifting whole communities out of cycles of poverty. Programmes were to be funded for 10 years.

Sure Start Local Programmes (SSLPs) were required to provide five core services: outreach and home visiting; support for families and parents; good-quality play/early learning/childcare; healthcare for children and parents; support for children (and their parents) with additional needs and/or disabilities. Though specific targets were set (for example, reduction in parents' smoking, higher percentage of parents in work or training, reduction in low birth weights, enhanced language development for 3-year-olds), the programmes were given relative freedom in how they implemented the core services. Unlike Children's Centres which were established from 2006, SSLPs were autonomous from local authority control, but required to work in partnership with local stakeholders such as health, social services, education, the voluntary and private sectors, community initiatives and parents.

The National Evaluation of Sure Start (NESS) reflected the SSLP holistic approach to intervention. The themed studies on which the following chapters are based focused on pivotal aspects of how the services for families with young children were delivered on the ground and how the infrastructures and ethos of programmes supported new ways of working.

References

Anning, A., Cottrell, D.J., Frost, N., Green, J. and Robinson, M. (2006) *Developing Multi-professional Teamwork for Integrated Children's Services*. Maidenhead: Open University Press.

Aubrey, C. (2007) *Leading and Managing in the Early Years*. London: Sage.

Bilson, A. (ed.) (2005) *Evidence-based Practice in Social Work*. London: Whiting and Birch.

Bishop, D.V.M. (2000) 'How does the brain learn language? Insights from the study of children with and without language impairment', *Developmental Medicine and Child Neurology*, 42: 133–42.

Blair, T. (1998) *The Third Way: New Politics for the New Century*. London: The Fabian Society.

Blair, M. and Hall, D. (2006) 'From health surveillance to health promotion: the changing focus in preventive children's services', *Archives of Disease in Childhood*, 91: 730–35.

Bronfenbrenner, U. (1979) *The Ecology of Human Development: Experiments by Nature and Design.* Cambridge, MA: Harvard University Press.

Cameron, A. and Lart, R. (2003) 'Factors promoting and obstacles hindering joint working: a systematic review of the research evidence', *Journal of Integrated Care,* 11 (2): 9–17.

DfEE (Department for Education and Employment) (1998) *Meeting the Childcare Challenge* (Green Paper). London: HMSO.

DfEE/QCA (Department for Education and Employment/Qualifications and Curriculum Authority) (2000) *Curriculum Guidance for the Foundation Stage.* London: Qualifications and Curriculum Authority.

DfES (Department for Education and Skills) (2002) *Birth to Three Matters: A Framework for Supporting Children in their Earliest Years.* London: HMSO.

DfES (Department for Education and Skills) (2003) *Every Child Matters.* London: HMSO.

DfES (Department for Education and Skills) (2004) *Every Child Matters: Change for Children.* London: HMSO.

DfES (Department for Education and Skills) (2005a) *Ten Year Strategy on Childcare.* London: HMSO.

DfES (Department for Education and Skills) (2005b) *Common Core of Skills and Knowledge for the Children's Workforce.* London: HMSO.

DfES/DoH (Department for Education and Skills and Department of Health) (2004) *The National Framework for Children, Young People and Maternity Services.* London: DoH.

DoH (Department of Health) (2004) *Choosing Health.* London: DoH.

Glass, N. (1999) 'Sure Start: the development of an early intervention programme for young children in the United Kingdom', *Children and Society,* 13: 257–64.

Glisson, C. and Hemmelgarn, A. (1998) 'The effects of organizational climate and interorganizational coordination on the quality and outcomes of children's service systems', *Child Abuse and Neglect,* 22(5): 401–21.

Hall, D.M.B. (1989) *Health for all Children: A Programme for Child Health Surveillance* (1st edition). Oxford: Oxford University Press.

Hallet, C. and Birchall, E. (1992) *Co-ordination and Child Protection: A Review of the Literature.* London: HMSO.

Karoly, L.A., Greenwood, P.W., Everingham, S.S., Hoube, J., Kilburn, M.R., Rydell, C.P., Sanders, M. and Chiesa, J. (1998) *Investing in our Children: What we Know and Don't Know about the Costs and Benefits of Early Childhood Interventions.* Santa Monica, CA: RAND.

Laming, H. (2003) *The Victoria Climbié Inquiry.* London: HMSO.

Melhuish, E. (2004) *A Literature Review of the Impact of Early Years Provision upon Young Children, with Emphasis Given to Children from Disadvantaged Backgrounds: Report to the Comptroller and Auditor General.* London: National Audit Office.

Melhuish, E. and Hall, D. (2007) 'The policy background to Sure Start', in J. Belsky, E. Melhuish and J. Barnes (eds) *The National Evaluation of Sure Start: Does area-based early intervention work?.* London: The Policy Press.

Morgan, P., Ghate, D. and Van der Merwe, A. (2004) *What Works in Parenting Support: A Review of the International Evidence.* London: DfES.

Olds, D.L. (2002) 'Prenatal and infancy home visiting by nurses: from randomized trials to community replication', *Behavioural Science*, 3: 153–72.

Olds, D.L., Kitzman, H., Cole, R., Robinson, J., Sidora, K., Luckey, D.W., Henderson, C.R. Jr., Hanks, C., Body, J. and Holmberg, J. (2004a) 'Effects of nurse visiting on maternal life course and child development: age 6 follow-up results of a randomized trial', *Pediatrics*, 114 (6): 1550–59.

Olds, D.L., Robinson, J., Pettitt, L., Luckey, D.W., Homberg, J., Ng, R.K., Isacks, K., Sheff, K. and Henderson, C.J. Jr. (2004b) 'Effects of home visits by paraprofessionals and by nurses: age 4 follow-up results of a randomized trial', *Pediatrics*, 114 (6): 1506–68.

Ramey, C.T. and Campbell, F.A. (1991) 'Poverty, early childhood education and academic competence: the Abecedarian experiment', in A. C. Huston (ed.) *Children in Poverty: Child Development and Public Policy*. Cambridge, MA: Cambridge University Press. 190–221.

Reynolds, A.J., Temple, J.A., Robertson, D.L. and Mann, E. A. (2001) 'Long-term effects of an early childhood intervention on educational achievement and juvenile arrest: a 15-year follow-up of low-income children in public schools', *Journal of American Medical Association*, 285: 2339–46.

Schweinhart, L.J., Barnes, H. and Weikhart, D. (eds) (1993) *Significant Benefits: The High/Scope Perry Pre-school Study through age 27*. Ypsilanti, MI: High/Scope Press.

Shonkoff, J.P. and Meisels, S.J. (eds) (2000) *Handbook of Early Childhood Intervention*. New York and Cambridge: Cambridge University Press.

Shonkoff, J.P. and Phillips, D.A. (2000) *From Neurons to Neighbourhoods: The Science of Early Childhood Development*. Washington, DC: National Academy Press.

Sloper, P. (2004) 'Facilitators and barriers for co-ordinated, multi-agency services', *Child: Care, Health and Development*, 30 (3): 571–80.

Tomlinson, K. (2003) *Effective Inter-agency Working: A Review of the Literature and Examples for Practice.* Slough: National Foundation for Educational Research.

Utting, D. (1999) *A Guide to Evidence Based Practice*. London: DfES.

Young, K., Ashby, D., Boaz, A. and Grayson, L. (2002) 'Social science and the evidence-based policy movement', *Social Policy and Society*, 1 (3): 215–24.

Suggested further reading

Health

Aynsley-Green, A., Barker, M., Burr, S., Macfarlane, A., Morgan, J., Sibert, J., Turner, T., Viner, R., Waterston, T. and Hall, D. (2000) 'Who is speaking for children and adolescents and for their health at policy level?', *British Medical Journal*, 321: 229–32.

Halfon, N., Russ, S. and Regalado, M. (2005) *The Life Course Health development Model: A Guide to Children's Health Care Policy and Practice: Zero to Three*. (Available at www.zerotothree.org)

Hall, D. and Elliman, D. (2006) *Health for All Children*, 4th edition. Oxford: Oxford University Press.

Making a difference in the lives of infants and toddlers and their families: the impacts of Early Head Start. (Available at www.headstartinfo.org/infocenter/ehs_tkit1.htm)

Social services

Fawcett, B., Featherstone, B. and Goddard, J. (2004) *Contemporary Child Care Policy and Practice*. Basingstoke: Palgrave MacMillan.

Frost, N. (2005) *Professionalism, Partnership and Joined-up Thinking: A Research Review of Frontline Working with Children*. Dartington: Research in Practice.

Hayden, C. (2007) *Children in Trouble: The Role of Families, Schools and Communities*. Basingstoke: Palgrave MacMillan.

Parton, N. (2006) *Safeguarding Children*. Basingstoke: Palgrave MacMillan.

Education and childcare

Anning, A. and Edwards, A. (2006) *Promoting Children's Learning from Birth to Five: Developing the New Early Years Professional*, 2nd edition. Maidenhead: Open University Press.

Dalhberg, G., Moss, P. and Pence, A. (2006) *Beyond Quality in Early Childhood Education and Care: Languages of Evaluation*. London: Routledge.

Nurse, A.D. (2007) *The New Early Years Professional: Dilemmas and Debates*. London: Routledge.

Pugh, G. and Duffy, B. (2006) *Contemporary Issues in the Early Years*, 4th edition. London: Paul Chapman/Sage.

Part 1

Establishing Appropriate
Sites for Service Delivery

Effective Communication and Engagement

Effective communication is pivotal to engaging users. It requires listening skills as well as the ability to talk in a language which people understand. Practitioners from all sectors, including the voluntary and private sectors, need to communicate with their colleagues by being open to distinctive approaches in child and family support and willing to explain their own approach. They need to lay aside traditional boundaries and hierarchies to do this, avoid jargon, and value what may be unfamiliar versions of childhood and family. The same applies to the interaction with families. In addition, practitioners need to be non-judgmental, focus on families' strengths rather than weaknesses, and build on what people *can* rather than what they cannot do.

Families have a choice about participating in services, and it is up to managers and practitioners to advertise, publicise and 'sell' what is on offer to them. The new practitioner in the children's workforce will be expected to write leaflets, posters, newsletter material, and work creatively – often at the behest of parent editors and organisers. They will be expected to get out on the streets to let people know about services, and to ask them what they want. It will no longer be enough to sit in an office and wait for 'clients'.

Parents will have a much bigger say in the kind of venues used for services in the future. Such services will be less bureaucratic and more family-friendly. They will need to be accessible to all families and to look welcoming and fun places. The message will be that children's services include a wide range of activities from the most informal to the highly specialised, from universal to targeted, for newborns to grandparents.

2 Getting Sure Start Started

Mog Ball

This chapter:

- describes the context in which Sure Start Local Programmes (SSLPs) got started
- discusses approaches SSLPs took to setting up and managing partnerships
- explores how SSLPs involved parents in partnerships
- explores the role of programme managers
- draws out key messages for children's centres.

Key questions:

- What dilemmas did SSLPs have to address in setting up and managing partnerships?
- How can parents be effectively involved in partnerships?
- What role do centre managers play in the smooth running of partnerships?
- What lessons can children's centres take from SSLPs' experiences of getting started?

The Secretary of State for Education and Employment, the Rt. Hon. David Blunkett and the Minister of State for Public Health, the Rt. Hon. Tessa Jowell announced the Sure Start programme together in 1999. Young children and their families were the future:

> Providers of services and support will work together in new ways that cut across old professional and agency boundaries and focus more successfully on family and community needs. Particular services, help and advice will often be brought together in a single place. Referral to other specialised services will be streamlined. In some cases, additional services will address unmet need. Sure Start will work with parents to help them nurture their children and stimulate their physical, social and intellectual development. In Whitehall and at regional level, cultural change and better coordination will underpin local efforts. (DfEE, 1999)

To many of those who had been working with young children and their families, this announcement was exciting. The involvement of central government in early years provision had been minimal in England. Local government had shown only a little more commitment, and that uneven. Until the late 1980s the most widespread experience for children under five had been in pre-school playgroups run by local voluntary groups. They used play as a basis for socialisation and learning. They relied on parents to become involved in supporting the group through fund-raising and as volunteer helpers. Local authorities supported the umbrella organisation, the Pre-School Playgroup Association, by funding authority-wide organisers, who trained staff and volunteers (McQuail and Pugh, 1995).

National voluntary organisations, like National Children's Home (NCH), Barnardos and the Children's Society, were also active in the local early years field, providing support through family centres situated in disadvantaged areas (often on behalf of the local authority and partly funded by them). They ran day care and other activities for children and parents. Local authorities often fulfilled their statutory duties to families with special needs through voluntary organisations – often local, small, unfunded, self-help groups. Although play and recreation were the responsibility of district councils, few employed staff directly for children's activities, the majority buying-in projects from voluntary organisations.

A handful of inner city local authorities had gone further, setting up nurseries and family centres, jointly funded by social services and the health or education authority. In rare examples, like Leeds, Kirklees and North Tyneside, the local government departments with a responsibility for young children had become a partnership and were co-ordinating their work. Families liked integrated services because it reduced a sense that they were being targeted by the Social Services Department, and more people used joined-up services on single sites (Smith, 1996; Makins, 1997).

But when Sure Start was announced, in the visionary, idealistic tones quoted, it demonstrated a new concern with an area that was almost a 'greenfield site'. Although governments elsewhere in Europe had taken an interest in the pre-school development of young citizens, in England the attitude remained that this was a period of child development when the privacy of the family held sway (Pugh and Duffy, 2006).

Managed by a partnership

The new Sure Start programmes were to be managed by a local partnership between agencies, organisations and individuals, especially parents, who had an interest in the well-being of children under four years old in the 'neighbourhood'. Neighbourhoods were to be small, perhaps one or two miles radius in urban areas, so that services would be easy for families to reach by walking and would make sense to the local community (DfEE, 1999).

There was a precedent for such partnerships in the early years field. Professionals working with young children had formed 'Under 5s (or 8s) Forums', informal and often unacknowledged groupings intended to co-ordinate local services. As part of the implementation of the Children Act (1989), some local authorities provided support to these voluntary structures. By 1997 local authorities were required to form Early Years Development Partnerships – subsequently Early Years Development and Childcare Partnerships (EYDCPs) – to plan their daycare and pre-school provision. These structures were influential for a period, since they were the mechanism which drew up the local plans for using central government funds directed at early years provision. Although they were serviced by local authority officers, decision-making in EYDCPs was spread across statutory, voluntary and private sectors.

Government guidance for Sure Start local programmes stipulated that Sure Start partnerships should comprise the key statutory agencies: health, education and social services, representatives from voluntary organisations, and representatives from the local community, including parents of young children. It described the members of this structure as residents and workers with a particular interest in the area and a knowledge of local communities. But it was also essential that the partnership was forged at a high managerial level, particularly for statutory and voluntary sector staff, who needed the support of their managers to give time to Sure Start. It was also important for community representatives and parents to have some support, such as training in committee work and confidence-building, so that they could speak confidently for others like themselves.

How to manage a partnership

The following good practice helped partnerships to function successfully:

- **an early agreement** between the chief executives of the main statutory bodies that this was a collaborative initiative for the benefit of children and families to which their departments were equally committed. This also meant a recognition that the funding for Sure Start was ring-fenced, not available to pay for services previously funded. The government required this local guarantee, but it was useful to have a meeting where senior managers acknowledged that they understood this. Senior managers also needed to give a commitment to staff involved in the partnership, backing them with the department's resources when necessary. For example, the partnership might need information held by the local health trust. Staff in the trust could be obstructive unless they had a clear directive that they should meet such requests.
- **a clear line of communication** from statutory members of the partnership to their local managers, through which they could report on progress in the partnership and the development of the programme, and represent their agency and its priorities.
- **a dedicated member of the partnership** from each statutory agency. A shifting membership, changing from week to week, was common and unhelpful. Partnerships worked best if they comprised individuals who got to know one another and the issues they were tackling.
- **voluntary sector representation** which was known and understood by all the relevant voluntary organisations in the area. This kind of sector approval was rarely sought, but always necessary. All voluntary organisations working with children in Sure Start neighbourhoods were in line to benefit from generous Sure Start funding. This put them in competition with one another. There was unequal competition between the larger, national voluntary organisations and small, local groups. To ensure that

all local organisations and the interested national voluntary sector were able to contribute, some mediation was useful. Local Councils for Voluntary Service (CVSs) and the National Council for Voluntary Child Care Organisations were in a good position to take this role.

- **a mechanism** to enable local parents to contribute to the discussion about plans for services and to the management of the programme. Sure Start guidance required this, but it needed commitment on the part of other partnership members to make it a reality.
- **being inclusive** and spreading the net widely meant discovering early on which subjects mattered to parents with young children living in the area and making sure that relevant expertise was within the partnership. It was disappointing to see how rarely housing officials were members of SSLP boards. When they were, the local programme benefited. The aim in one which did have a housing member on the partnership was: 'To ensure that no baby coming home from hospital will sleep in an unheated room.' Women's aid groups, local community arts organisations and the police were among others who proved helpful contributors.

As partnerships got underway and began to plan the programme, subgroups were formed to take forward particular aspects. These working groups commonly reflected the five core Sure Start service areas: outreach and home visiting; support to families and parents; good quality play, learning and childcare experiences for children; primary and community health and advice; support for people with special needs. However, there were other issues like buildings, play areas, staffing, finance, transport or the needs of minority communities that generated working groups.

Getting parents onto partnerships

Some partnerships established a sub-group for parents only, at which they received training and support to participate in meetings. Parent representatives were elected from this group to the partnership board. These processes took time, and yet the partnership was under pressure to produce the plan and put it in place within six months. A member of such a sub-group reported: 'I don't think parents were equal to it until their own network was formed ... so we ended up getting input from parents rather too late in the process, and when we did invite them to contribute there was a good deal of tension in the atmosphere' (Ball, 2002: 17). As discussed in Chapter 5, the requirement for parent members of the partnership, and for consultation with local parents, was an important aspect of the empowering parents. It was not about telling parents what to do, but enabling them to take control and do things for themselves.

The average number of parents on partnership boards investigated by National Evaluation of Sure Start (NESS) was two, but in some cases parents formed the majority. Where numbers were small, parents felt isolated. Parents could be prevented from contributing to partnership business because:

- the language used, particularly professional jargon, excluded them;
- bureaucracy grew quickly, with partnerships generating large amounts of paper;
- the demand was onerous, and the responsibility (each partnership had at least £1 million to spend each year, quite apart from any money it would be using for buildings) meant that membership took up more and more time;
- the feeling that professional agencies, especially the council or health trusts, but sometimes voluntary organisations, had already decided how the Sure Start funding would be spent;
- community divisions, which meant that some parents excluded themselves. This was quite common, and quite difficult for outsiders to understand. There were distinctive communities within SSLP areas. People living in some streets did not associate with people living in other streets, even though these might be close to one another and appear similar.

In the kind of disadvantaged areas in which SSLPs were located, residents had become used to government initiatives which 'consulted' with local people. Such exercises were considered tokenistic, inadequate for assessing the real needs and feelings in communities, and merely carried out to provide a veneer of popular support for policies superimposed from Whitehall or the Town Hall. Sure Start partnerships tried to overcome such preconceptions to get parents to participate. But parents of young children have a lot to do and many found they could not make a regular commitment.

Consulting with parents

The essence of good consultation is to allow people to give information and express their views, to pay close attention to what they say and to act on it where possible. Good consultation will enable services to be designed which meet the needs of people so that they are more likely to use them. Hearing about the experience of users can indicate where and how services can be improved. It is a way of discovering information that only local parents know about, such as community divisions. Genuine consultation treats parents as customers, with status and rights, rather than as passive recipients of services. It sets up a partnership between parents and others interested in the well-being and education of their child, but for this to be effective, there must be mutual respect and understanding from each of the partners. They must be in continual dialogue and learn to share their distinctive expertise and information with each other.

Consultation also enables the design of services to be sensitive to the needs of specific groups. But perhaps the best reason of all for SSLPs to consult with parents was that it avoided expensive mistakes. The failure of past social policies were directly linked to lack of public consultation – the development of high-rise housing in the 1960s, for example. If families in Sure Start areas were able to tell the partnership what they wanted, they were more likely to use it when it was provided.

Finally, consulting with parents was a way to give them information about the new programme. This was one of the first targets for the partnership: to inform 100 per cent of parents of children aged under four about Sure Start services. Preliminary payments funded the fun days and parties, leaflets and posters and many other activities, providing opportunities to ask parents to complete survey forms and say what they wanted the SSLP to provide.

The main challenges to consulting were the limited time and expertise available, the difficulty of getting a large enough group of parents to respond, and the problem of involving all groups of parents. Many young parents, though committed to bringing up their child or children, did not identify themselves primarily as parents, and were not always clear that consultation was relevant to them. Parents from minority ethnic groups were cynical about attempts to consult with them, in the light of previous experience:

'Past efforts have tended to be *ad hoc* and piecemeal, and have therefore sometimes been discredited in black and minority ethnic communities. As a consequence, renewed attempts at consultation may provoke expressions of anger and dissatisfaction. That may be an unavoidable test of commitment before it is possible to achieve a new level of understanding and to begin a more constructive and sustainable dialogue' (DoH/DoE, 1996).

Just as there could be problems when consulting individual parents in ensuring that everyone's voice was heard, there were dangers in consulting some voluntary groups and assuming that they spoke for the whole voluntary sector. And community organisations were not always representative of the whole community. This was particularly true in areas with diverse populations, where there were sometimes several voluntary organisations representing what appeared to be a coherent minority population. In such situations it was essential that collaborations were not confined to a single local group, and a certain amount of investigation was necessary to make sure that all interests were included.

Involving the voluntary sector

Good practice in involving the voluntary sector includes:

- **an early approach** to small groups to discuss the subject and methods for the consultation, to ask advice and explore the terms of which they would be willing to collaborate.
- **training for staff** in voluntary groups about the purpose and methods of the consultation.
- **a contract** for each group detailing the tasks to be undertaken and the remuneration to be received for carrying them out.
- **feedback** to groups on the results of consultation and the use to which they will be put.
- **crediting** of all groups who have contributed in any published reports.

Relationships in partnerships

To start with, Sure Start partnerships had no infrastructure of their own: no offices, no computers, no pens, no personnel. Government guidance asked for one member of the partnership be appointed 'lead' for purposes of communication. Partnerships did not do this using any formal process: 'The lead partner was chosen because it had the personnel and time to do the Delivery Plan and cope with the extra work' (Partnership member, SSLP; Ball, 2002).

Participation in partnerships was a burden for all agencies, taking more time and requiring more effort than had been anticipated. They could become dominated by one member, usually the lead partner, which had considerable power to dictate the contents of the programme. A parent who was a member of a Sure Start partnership said: 'The most difficult part of the planning process was knowing that no matter what was said, the agenda was already written. A small group on the partnership had made all the decisions' (Sure Start parent; Ball, 2002).

The nature of relationships in the partnership was the most significant factor in setting up the local programme. Where statutory and voluntary agencies were able to set aside their own interests and respond to the views of local people, they worked well. Relationships on partnerships tended to settle once the planning process was over. Statutory partners became more responsive to the results of consultation with families.

However, both statutory and voluntary sector partners often experienced conflicts of interest. Partnership members were expected to put the interests of their own organisation aside in the interest of children and families in the neighbourhood. But partnerships commissioned services from partnership members, and the substantial resources available had the potential to divide as well as unite: 'I went to meetings for a while but (another voluntary organisation) had its foot in the door and it looked as though they were going to get the funding. It didn't really seem worth the effort, really' (Chair, local voluntary organisation; Ball, 2002).

The programme manager

The appointment of a Sure Start manager was the first step in supplying some infrastructure, and their arrival made it easier for partnerships to complete their plan and set up a programme. The Sure Start manager role was new for the early years field. Project planning, management of an expanding workforce, handling large budgets and development experience were more useful skills in programme managers than experience of work with children and families. The pool of people with the skills to manage complex, multi-functional local initiatives was small.

Different skills were needed for writing the delivery plan and implementing it. Some new programme managers felt that it was important to arrive when the plan was written, and so to be 'untainted' by the process of negotiating the delivery plan with partners. Others reported that their job might have been easier if they had been involved earlier in the planning process: 'It is very difficult to come into an area and to have this role of guiding everyone, without a background in every professional area. You are between everybody – the members of the partnership, the partnership and the parents, different groups of parents. Sometimes you wonder where your authority is coming from' (Sure Start manager; Ball, 2002).

The programme manager was employed by the partnership but developed the SSLP with the community. This could mean contradictory demands, and managers reported having to represent community preferences and fight with their employers for them. In successful programmes a good deal of trust was placed in the programme manager by the partnership – far more than would be usual for a statutory employee on equivalent salary levels. The partnership, like the management committee of a voluntary organisation, relied on the programme manager to develop the programme with their support, rather than tell them what to do. Where this kind of trusting relationship was not forthcoming, managers felt frustrated.

Key messages

It took Sure Start local programmes a long time to get up and running and to make all planned services available. In many areas this was because it took a long time to complete or convert buildings, so there were insufficient or inappropriate bases from which to deliver services (see Chapter 3).

Even where a partnership was well-balanced, where members understood that the needs of their own agency or organisation were secondary to those of families in the area, and where consultation with families was established quickly, there could be unforeseen difficulties: finding suitably skilled staff; persuading practitioners to change their working styles or practices; incorporating existing services into the SSLP.

Recruitment difficulties hampered over half of the programmes studied. A member of one partnership reported: 'Demands for specific skills are high. There aren't enough skilled people to go round – and we couldn't recruit people because there were no buildings to put them in' (Ball, 2002). In some areas SSLPs were unable to appoint skilled workers in short supply nationally: speech and language specialists, midwives and health visitors. Where this happened, planning for services had to be revisited with a resulting time lag in services. This had an impact on community commitment. The transformation of staff from different backgrounds into a Sure Start team was complex, and preparing them for 'joined-up' working was time-consuming.

Some services based on existing provision were easier to get going, like drop-in centres and libraries. But even though programmes could get services going quickly to maintain parents' interest, they were reluctant to do so without consulting parents. Because they wanted parents to feel ownership of the programme, extra time was needed to set up services.

The most significant factor in successful implementation of Sure Start local programmes was the nature of the partnership. Progress was most marked in areas where members contributed materially to the design and development of the programme. Where partners put the interests and needs of families before those of their own organisations and agencies, and listened and responded to parents' views, they had a workable programme within 12 to 18 months. But even then unforeseen events and obstacles arose. Despite clear guidance from the government's Sure Start Unit, and flexible and very generous resources, the establishment of fully functioning Sure Start local programmes was a lengthier process than local partnerships could have anticipated.

References

Ball, M. (2002) *Getting Sure Start Started*. Nottingham: Department for Education and Skills/National Evaluation of Sure Start.

DfEE (Department for Education and Employment) (1999) *Sure Start: A Guide for Trailblazers*. Sudbury: DfES.

DoH/DoE (Department of Health/Department of Education) (1996) *Race, Culture and Community Care*. London: HMSO.

McQuail, S. and Pugh, G. (1995) *Effective Organisation of Early Childhood Services*. London: National Children's Bureau.

Makins, V. (1997) *Not Just a Nursery: Multi-agency Early Years Centres in Action*. London: National Children's Bureau.

Pugh, G. and Duffy, B. (eds) (2006) *Contemporary Issues in the Early Years: Working Collaboratively for Children*, 3rd edition. London: Paul Chapman in association with Coram Family.

Smith, T. (1996) *Family Centres and Bringing Up Young Children*. London: HMSO.

Suggested further reading

Ball, M. (2002) *Getting Sure Start Started*. Nottingham: Department for Education and Skills/National Evaluation of Sure Start.

Pugh, G. and Duffy, B. (eds) (2006) *Contemporary Issues in the Early Years: Working Collaboratively for Children*, 3rd edition. London: Paul Chapman in association with Coram Family.

3 Sure Start Buildings and Venues

Mog Ball

This chapter:

- discusses the central importance of buildings and venues in the delivery of Sure Start Local Programme (SSLP) services
- explores the characteristics and patterns of usage of buildings used by SSLPs
- discusses the advantages and disadvantages of different models of building design and use
- concludes with implications of why buildings matter for children's centres.

Key questions:

- Why are buildings important for the success of services for families and children?
- How did SSLPs make innovative use of buildings and spaces?
- What are the pros and cons of professionals sharing spaces for their work?
- What lessons can children's centres learn from the experiences of SSLPs in their use of buildings and venues?

Creating services and reconfiguring existing services for children and families have implications for the places from which they are delivered. SSLPs were about changing services. The fact that this would mean re-thinking service location was reflected in two elements of the programme: substantial capital resources made available to each SSLP area, from which they could finance buildings; and the requirement that all programmes provide services through outreach and home visiting. This chapter, based on the themed study of buildings (Ball and Niven, 2005), looks at these aspects of SSLPs and explores how services can be made as accessible as possible for families.

Sure Start services needed to be clearly signposted, welcoming, easy to reach and flexible for family use. Programmes were to work in new ways, cutting across professional boundaries through 'joined-up' working, and co-locating staff in one building, where they could deliver advice and help to families, could be a useful part of this process. Sure Start premises served functions such as:

- informal space for parents and children to meet, socialise and interact;
- structured and informal space for children to be cared for and to play – day care, crèche, play group and play space;
- bases for practitioners and professionals – office, meeting and other support facilities;
- venues for regular group activities like clinics, classes and courses;
- facilities for individual work with parents and children.

Knowledge and resources

In 1999 there were few buildings in the UK designed to fulfil the functions outlined above. There was no tradition of developing such buildings and little experience of what buildings for 'early years services' might involve, other than the work, pioneered by a small number of architects, in designing sites for pre-school education and care such as in the Reggio Emilia approach in Northern Italy (Ceppi and Zini, 1998; Dudek, 2000).

Where buildings had been used as integrated centres in the UK, they had often begun with different purposes – usually as schools. The experience of building specifically for very young children had largely been gleaned through the building of day nurseries. Even this was limited, and grew rapidly only once SSLPs had begun and the Neighbourhood Nursery Initiative (NNI) was launched in SSLP areas at the end of 2000. Like Sure Start, the NNI focused on disadvantaged areas and aimed to provide an increase in childcare places. The NNI was funded by private enterprise, using links with local businesses (a Public/Private Finance Initiative) but administered through Early Years Development and Childcare Partnerships (EYDCPs) (see Chapter 2). The NNI and SSLP initiatives were closely linked and together led to an exponential growth in buildings for use by families with young children.

The double focus of SSLPs – on the child and on the family – presented new challenges for those responsible for designing the buildings. All SSLPs had at least £750,000 available for capital projects, and were encouraged by government to seek additional funding for larger projects (by collaborations with the privately-financed NNI, and from sources like the New Deal for Communities and European Funds). The Sure Start approach emphasised that parents and other community members were to be involved in the planning, management and delivery of the building developments. Many local programmes found it easier to get parental involvement in building plans than in other aspects of the programme: local people were more interested in practical, concrete projects than the somewhat vaguer notion of 'services' (which some thought referred to buses, or church).

Building and converting is a process often beset by difficulties and delays. For SSLPs these included problems in identifying buildings appropriate for renovation, or land available to build on; rapid increases in the cost of land, and other land and lease negotiation difficulties, which had to be dealt with by local partnerships with little expertise in building projects. The burden fell upon Sure Start managers, and many of them described the capital process as 'a nightmare'. One said, 'The requirements of the capital programme feel like another job on top of the full-time job you have as a programme manager' (Ball and Niven, 2005). Although many of the difficulties encountered were specific to the Sure Start capital process, it is likely that the management of any development for children's services will meet similar challenges.

One solution was the appointment of a full-time member of staff to handle the day-to-day elements of building development. In some areas a capital team led by the local authority made good progress. This model will apply to Children's Centres, which are managed by local authorities. But in 2004, SSLPs reported that local authority project managers could be ignorant of and insensitive to the needs of programmes dealing with young children and families: 'His priorities were different from ours – he was constantly telling us that things were going to happen at the last minute. But we were an operational programme, trying to deliver services to families. We needed to know what was going to happen so that we could inform users' (Ball and Niven, 2005). However, where SSLPs increased their capital with funding from non-Sure Start sources, the key to the success of complicated arrangements was to let the local authority do the commissioning for the building.

Characteristics of buildings used for Sure Start services

Although an SSLP neighbourhood could be quite a small geographic area, especially when it was in a large city, programmes were using, on average, nine buildings from which to deliver services. Most of these were shared with other agencies, chosen because families were already familiar with them, because they were close to family housing or, sometimes, because it took a long time to get family-specific buildings up and running. However, almost all SSLPs had one building that was dedicated to the delivery of Sure Start services (often called the 'centre'). This was either purpose-built or a conversion or refurbishment of an existing building. In a few cases the SSLP decided not to construct but use existing community sites. They included urban programmes that could not find affordable space to build on, and rural programmes that covered such a wide area that it made more sense to spend capital on smaller-scale refurbishments. But in at least one SSLP – a large peripheral estate that had been the subject of investment by regeneration programmes since the 1970s – the partnership made a decision that a centre was unnecessary and unhelpful to the programme philosophy of outreach and empowerment. In this case the programme was able to become operational quickly, since it was not pre-occupied with building development.

Patterns of building use

SSLPs used buildings as:

- **Hub and satellites:** This was the most prevalent model and involved a single Sure Start building and a number of smaller, satellite buildings distributed around the area. The centre provided office accommodation for core staff.
- **Two hubs:** Some SSLP areas divided clearly into two parts, perhaps divided by a major road, perhaps because the programme covered two distinct estates, or perhaps because patterns of settlement meant that there were identifiable and separate communities. In these cases SSLPs tried to develop two buildings of equal significance, delivering a similar range of services.
- **Three or more hubs:** This pattern was extended in those SSLP areas that covered a group of distinct, smaller communities. For example, three former mining villages, three miles apart, had a Sure Start building in each, one newly built and two refurbished. In the central area of a city the SSLP covered four neighbourhoods, each with a distinct ethnic community, and developed a Sure Start building in each.
- **A large number of sites, with no hub:** The model was commonest in rural areas, or in programmes with a strong empowering, community-development ethos, where the emphasis was on outreach and home visiting to deliver services.

Advantages and disadvantages of different patterns

SSLPs reported benefits from all these models, largely because they had developed them in response to local history, geography and need. The single, newly-built or converted Sure Start centre provided an outward and visible sign of the programme, with its development and launch an opportunity for publicity and the generation of community interest. Such buildings symbolised the multi-agency aspect of Sure Start, and encouraged joined-up working and easy access to a range of services. In their design they could embody a positive message about young children and families and their importance to the community.

Two hubs could also gain attention, but SSLPs had to be careful about the perceived fairness of what was on offer. Where there were distinctly divided communities in an SSLP neighbourhood, two Sure Start buildings could encourage cross-over between the communities. Such buildings could also respond to diversity and neighbourhood identity and could develop a strong local flavour.

However, the absence of a big central building allowed the SSLPs without one to avoid an 'institutional' profile. These programmes drew on the familiarity factor, using buildings that were already liked and established in the community. In several Sure Start areas parents reported that they had attachments to such buildings. These included family rooms attached to schools, nurseries and family centres, and were often small, single-storey structures, and quite unprepossessing. Sometimes they had been used by generations of parents, and those interviewed remembered being brought to them in their own childhood.

Sharing buildings

SSLPs were collaborating with many partners in the development of premises. Collaboration could occur at various stages of building development and included sharing the cost and management of construction; sharing the continuing maintenance costs and sharing the buildings for work and the delivery of services. On the whole, sharing led to benefits for all parties.

Sharing with a school

Schools often offer space for extension. They have the advantage of being a place that parents may be using already and will probably continue to use as the children grow. There was evidence that Sure Start premises based in schools worked best when the school's head worked with the SSLP partnership from the outset. When both shared the vision of an integrated building, the SSLP spaces did not look like 'add-ons' from inside or outside the buildings. But to achieve this it was essential that there was close liaison from the very beginning of the Sure Start planning process. In one area where the Sure Start building was an extension to a primary school, which also included a community nursery, the Sure Start manager felt that the Sure Start capital had been a small contribution to a large project to provide 'wrap-around' facilities at the school. She felt that it was seen as an insignificant add-on by the education authority. However, there are benefits for early years services in being part of a community school development. The school is visible, easily accessible and particularly convenient for the parents of post-Sure Start children. Other services are located there. But the whole development needs to be integrated into the community, and until that happens the early years services can experience difficulties in establishing an identity and forging a relationship with families.

Sharing with a health centre

Delivering early years services from health settings has very real advantages. Parents are likely to know the space from attending child health clinics, collecting baby milk, visiting the dentist or the speech and language therapist. Health clinics are acceptable to families from ethnic minority communities. In one area an SSLP found that Bengali husbands would allow their wives to attend language classes when they were offered at a health centre, but not elsewhere. The drawback to these buildings can be their institutional appearance (which does not send strong messages about young children in terms of colour, toys or general presentation) and their limited space, which means that several activities often taken place in the same room.

Sharing with a community organisation

Several SSLPs collaborated with community organisations to create buildings for the use of all local residents. Such buildings offered facilities like community cafés. The general management of areas like reception, and office booking were the responsibility of the wider building management. There was evidence that tensions could arise in such buildings, particularly over who had first call on the building's facilities. In one case a Sure Start home visiting team had taken over a community craft room which was no longer available for hiring out, with the result that income was not being generated from it. Community spaces were predominantly used for activities for older children and teenagers, and this could result in arguments about the clearing up of equipment and the state in which rooms were left. Smoking was a cause of tension, which reduced when it was banned in public spaces in 2007. On the benefit side, sharing spaces with community organisations gave the SSLPs concerned a rich source of community volunteers.

Sharing with a voluntary sector family centre

Where a family centre had been operating in a neighbourhood for some time, had established a good reputation locally, and was trusted by families, the addition of extra facilities for young children was absorbed seamlessly to mutual benefit. The buildings were very evidently for children, often with conspicuous outdoor play facilities, murals and other decoration that emphasised the purpose. Family centre and SSLP users passed through the same reception area into shared premises where the facilities for each were indistinguishable because all were child-centred. Although more than one organisation might operate in the building, the families who used them saw one 'joined-up' facility. These building developments were the ones that most resembled the high-quality centres for children and families available in some European countries (Dudek, 2000; Thornton and Brunton, 2005).

Sharing with a nursery

This common model for sharing was encouraged by the Neighbourhood Nursery Initiative. Although it made sense as a collaboration, the effectiveness of co-location depended on the willingness of staff to get to know one another, integrate and 'join-up'. Some nurseries kept a very separate identity and had little contact with the SSLP (and even had few families in common). Others were fully integrated, with the nursery manager undertaking a significant role in management decisions about the whole building.

Making sharing work

- Sharing was easier for SSLPs when they were the dominant partner in financing and managing a building.
- Sharing worked best when the agencies working alongside the SSLP were also working with children and where the age-group was not too far removed from the early years. Staff tended to have a similar outlook, could offer support to one another, and there was potential for overlap in services. Parents and children could move between all the services in the building.
- Ancillary staff were central to the success of sharing. Difficulties arose when caretakers were unco-operative – which was reported in situations of sharing with community organisations and schools.

In one multi-functional centre, to which an SSLP had contributed £1.2 million and which it shared with a health centre, a job centre, a library and an information centre, caretaking staff were reported as disliking young children: 'They are anxious about mess' (Manager; Ball and Niven, 2005). Such staff needed to be informed about services for young children and trained in working with them.
- Preliminary introductions and protocols needed to be established by management of all agencies using a building, to enable collaboration to proceed smoothly. SSLPs noted that regular staff and user meetings were required: 'It stops little grumbles becoming major issues' (Manager; Ball and Niven, 2005).

Buildings that users will want to use

What can we learn from SSLP buildings about what attracts families to buildings and the services in them? There were three aspects to attraction: external appearance, internal facilities, and the overall 'feel' of the building.

External appearance

Sure Start buildings in prominent positions raised the profile of the local programme. But there was evidence that buildings which did not stand out from the surroundings were liked by parents as well. For example, in one area the Sure Start centre was originally a block of six flats, exactly like those in which local families were living. In another it was a former dance hall whose key features had been retained; another was a 17th-century listed building where historical features had to be retained. These local associations were liked by families.

Also interesting were the buildings that aimed at sustainability – an appropriate aim given their role with new generations: 'The emphasis in our new building is sustainability ... There is no car parking, but space for bikes outside and buggies inside' (Manager; Ball and Niven, 2005). Car parking was considered to detract from the impact of buildings, with parents wishing spaces for parking to be behind buildings and less visible (but staff liked car parks better than parents did). One building with extensive parking was described as 'looking like a supermarket' (Parent; Ball and Niven, 2005). Several SSLPs noted that the spaces outside the buildings were important, and many had used these to develop wildlife areas. Visible outdoor play facilities were important too, not only for the children to play but also to signal the purpose of the building. Some SSLPs had drawn on guidance from organisations like Learning Through Landscapes (www.ltl.org.uk) to plan and develop high-quality outdoor play and learning areas. To emphasise this, and to mark their difference from typical public service buildings, many SSLP buildings were painted brightly. In one area an SSLP centre on the site of a former youth club (which had burned down) was painted purple and orange, with blue shutters and yellow window frames: 'You can't miss us,' directed a member of the staff (Ball and Niven, 2005). Many buildings were decorated with murals.

Security is a significant consideration in all buildings used by young children, and SSLPs had to keep a balance between protecting children and being open and welcoming to families. Where buildings include a nursery or other day care facilities, they are inspected by Ofsted before registration and judged against a set of standards, one of which requires that 'the premises are safe, secure and suitable for their purpose' (DfES, 2000). Concern was expressed about vandalism because Sure Start buildings are in disadvantaged areas, but most SSLPs reported that fears of damage to buildings had not been realised.

Internal facilities

The use of internal space depended on function: administration (office space); service delivery (meeting and interview rooms); spaces for parents (cafés, lounges); and spaces for children (nurseries, crèches, play areas). Even where a building was largely administrative, and used mostly by staff, SSLPs reported that the building could make a significant impression on families. For example, in one area a manager described how being based in the same building had improved communication between staff: 'We've achieved a wonderful level of joined-up working. Relationships between staff are very rich. Everyone gives and gets a great deal from one another. Parents share in this – they have richer relationships with staff themselves. The Sure Start building sends a message that we complement and enhance one another. The agencies are not in competition here' (Manager; Ball and Niven, 2005).

The reception area sent the clearest message to users, and that message needed to be 'welcome'. Parents liked to be able to see what was happening in the building before entering it. It helped if there were people in reception to welcome visitors and explain to them what went on. Other popular features were easy access and storage for pushchairs (many SSLPs had underestimated the space required for these); cafés and relaxation space (though poorly-planned cafés in reception areas could make them crowded and difficult to negotiate); good-quality toys for children, the sort that cannot be afforded by most families; soft play areas; and light, bright colours.

Features of successful reception areas include:

- Clear signs showing where to go.
- Limited amounts of written information (parents find displays with large numbers of leaflets off-putting and 'official').
- Lots of natural light.
- A café corner adding to the friendly feel.
- An informal and professional (but not 'official') ethos.
- Clear routes into the building.
- Open doors where possible.
- Shared spaces for parents and staff.
- Work and social activity equally visible.

Many Sure Start buildings revealed problems only once they were in use. In one case these were bad enough for the programme to stop using the building. More common were minor problems, like insufficient storage space (especially in the day care areas of buildings), insufficient room for staff (including no room for staff to relax, although many SSLPs expected staff to use the communal areas, such as kitchens), and poor routing through buildings (so that, for example, it was necessary to cross a crèche room to reach toilets).

Experience showed that integrated spaces worked best, so that Sure Start activities inhabited the whole building, and staff, children and parents felt at home while respecting one another's territory – offices for staff, communal areas for parents. All internal spaces worked best if they were linked to the main focus of Sure Start: small children. This was evident in areas where integrated services had been in existence before Sure Start. In these areas, previous experience of what works in offering services to families had resulted in some innovative design features, for example, incorporating water, sand and other play materials into the structure.

Parents liked intimacy in internal spaces – as shown by the popularity of single-storey, domestic-type structures, often with one room divided into areas for conversation, children's play and so on. Though Sure Start centres were catering for larger numbers, the most successful still achieved a domestic feel by the use of alcoves and other design features. Where parents had been involved in designing and decorating Sure Start buildings – not only choosing colour schemes and furniture, but actually wielding paint brushes and tools – they had a sense of pride in the building and commitment to it.

The 'feel' of a building

Much of the atmosphere of an attractive building was created by the attitude of the staff and other users. Parents at one local programme commented, 'It's not the space that really matters, it's the people inside' (Ball and Niven, 2005). The informal areas and communal spaces proved key to the opportunities for interaction between people, offering support-type facilities like kitchens, utility rooms with washing machines and dryers, and community cafés. Too much visible office space and bureaucratic activity could destroy this informality. The 'drop-in' atmosphere of centres which worked enabled practitioners to interact with families on an equal basis, and not the hierarchical one that parents dislike. Successful buildings enabled such interaction to flourish, and SSLPs reported that informal interaction increases the likelihood of parents disclosing difficulties to workers.

Key messages

SSLPs added significant numbers of buildings to the stock available for public services in a very short period. On the whole, these buildings avoided the stigma attached to public buildings and were not often seen as 'official'. All sorts of premises were adapted and made to work, with attention to a few basic rules about planning, sharing and adapting. Some Sure Start buildings revealed problems only when they were in use, which suggested that more and better consultation was needed before major projects were undertaken. Being consulted about the design and appearance of buildings increased a sense of ownership by users. Imaginative consultation methods, using community arts or Planning for Real®[1] gave families the most interesting experiences. But being consulted and ignored or over-ruled is disappointing and alienating. This happened in some Sure Start areas and resulted in lasting resentment among families.

Buildings are significant to public services, sending messages about the relationship between services and users. SSLPs began the process of developing buildings for children and families, but what they produced does not constitute a clear, collective, easily-recognised statement about the national commitment to giving small children the best start in life. This leaves plenty of space for children's centres to fill with distinctive, imaginative and exciting buildings.

Note

1 Planning for Real® is a process of community consultation offered by the Neighbourhood Initiatives Foundation which involves local people in making models of their community (www.nif.co.uk/planningforreal/).

References

Ball, M. and Niven, L. (2005) *Buildings in Sure Start Local Programmes*. Nottingham: DfES.

Ceppi, G. and Zini, M. (1998) *Children, Spaces, Relations: Meta Project for an Environment for Young Children*. Milan: Domus Academy Research Center.

DfES (Department of Education and Skills) (2000) *National Standards for Under Eights Day Care and Childminding*. (Available at www.childcarelink.gov.uk/standards.asp)

Dudek, M. (2000) *Kindergarten Architecture*. London: Spon.

Thornton, I. and Brunton, P. (2005) *Understanding the Reggio Approach*. London: David Fulton.

Suggested further reading

CABE (Commission for the Built Environment) (2003) *Creating Excellent Buildings: A Guide for Clients*. (Available at www.cabe.org.uk)

DfES (Department for Education and Skills) (2004) *Building for Sure Start: Integrated Provision for Under Fives*. (Produced in association with the Commission for the Built Environment (CABE), available at www.surestart.gove.uk/publications/index)

Ryder-Richardson, G. (2006) *Creating a Space to Grow: The Process of Developing your Outdoor Learning Environment*. London: David Fulton.

Part 2

Intervening in People's Lives

The Ethics of Social Engineering

The vision of Sure Start was that communities, by being involved in the programme, would engineer improvements in the lives of individuals, particularly of parents and families. People would gain control of their own lives, and power in local decision-making about their neighbourhood. The vision built on a tradition of community development which had been established for some time in some Sure Start areas, underpinned by central government initiatives to improve structural features in these areas: better housing, health care, educational and training opportunities, and family support systems.

Sure Start promoted the importance of parenting young children – which traditionally had not been a high-status activity, either domestically or as a career. It celebrated young children and their potential as the future of communities. As the custodians of that future generation of young children, parents were to be valued. However, the role of fathers in this process tended to be under-valued, both in the implementation of the programme and in the evaluation of its effectiveness. A predominantly female workforce tended to overlook the positive role of fathers and to underestimate both their influence on their children's lives and the contribution they could make to the programmes.

Fathers perceived Sure Start as 'women's territory'. Many professionals assumed that fathers would be absent from households in disadvantaged areas, or, if present, played little part in childcare, or, at the most extreme, caused problems within the family (for example, through violence, criminality or substance abuse). Yet research shows that where fathers are positively involved with children, their involvement was associated with better peer relationships, fewer behaviour problems, lower criminality and substance abuse, and higher education and occupational aspirations (Pleck and Masciadrelli, 2004).

There was also an assumption in the Sure Start vision that 'inclusive' services would satisfy the needs of all elements in diverse communities, reflecting the complexities of tuning into the needs of varied populations in contemporary Britain. But there was inadequate monitoring of the take-up of services by and preferences of different ethnic groups. And perhaps the challenges of meeting their needs was simply too daunting. Whatever the reasons, this was a disappointing aspect of Sure Start local programmes and a challenge to be confronted by professionals responsible for children's services.

People are already experts in their own lives and have networks and support systems – some of which are based on informal and faith groups. Professional staff can learn a great deal from tapping into such groups and individuals and working with them. The position of the workforce should be to stand shoulder to shoulder with them, rather than to assume a position of superiority. Public service is about serving people in all their diversity.

Reference

Pleck, J.H. and Masciadrelli, B.P. (2004) 'Paternal involvement by US residential fathers: levels, sources and consequences', in M.E. Lamb (ed.), *The Role of the Father in Child Development*, 4th edition Hoboken, NJ: John Wiley.

4 'The Elephant on the Sofa': Sure Start and Black and Minority Ethnic Populations

Gary Craig[1]

This chapter:

- gives a full account of deprivation among black and minority ethnic populations in the UK, and its impact on children
- critiques the attention paid to ethnicity and diversity by Sure Start Local Programmes (SSLPs) and by early years strategies at every level
- examines 12 SSLP areas with varying populations, and through this gives examples of practice, both good and bad, to meet the needs of minority groups
- includes recommendations for children's centres.

Key questions:

- Why are there links between ethnicity and poverty in the UK?
- Why did Sure Start local programmes find it so difficult to address the needs of minority groups effectively?
- How can practitioners find out more about the various populations in their locality?
- How can children's centres provide services which are sensitive to the needs of black and ethnic minority groups?

Background

The McPherson Inquiry, set up to investigate the death of Steven Lawrence, made recommendations both for the conduct of the police in relation to black and minority ethnic (BME) populations, and for the practice of all agencies delivering services to BME groups. In 2003, the Home Secretary publicly reminded welfare agencies that they should pay more serious attention to the terms of the Race Relations Amendment Act 2000, enacted in response to McPherson, such as the duty to promote race equality. Since then, there have been the Blofeld Inquiry into racism in the National Health Service, (a response to the death while being restrained of Michael Bennett, a black psychiatric in-patient); charges of racism in the prison service (after the murder of Zahid Mubarek in Feltham Young Offenders Institution by a white psychopathic man with whom he was forced to share a cell); further accusations of widespread racism against the probation service and the police; the failure of most Mental Health Trusts even to develop a race equality policy; and, early in 2007, the announcement by Trevor Phillips, outgoing chair of the Commission for Racial Equality, that he was instituting a formal inquiry into practices within the Department of Health.

The issue of racial discrimination within welfare services is thus on the public policy agenda and there is allegedly a serious political and policy commitment to addressing the needs of BME communities (Craig, 2007). In this context, the Sure Start intervention – probably the most generously-financed and targeted social policy initiative of the New Labour Government elected in 1997 – might be expected to give ethnicity a central place. Astonishingly, however, an analysis of the policy documentation issued at national, regional and local levels, of the work of the National Evaluation programme (NESS), and of the work of local programmes, shows that ethnicity was rarely a central consideration in the way the programme as a whole was developed, put into practice, or evaluated. This represented, for BME populations at least, a substantial wasted opportunity.

NESS had identified that there was a minority ethnic population of 20 per cent or more of the targeted area population in 38 per cent of the first 250 SSLP areas (at a time when minorities represented about 8 per cent of the total UK population). SSLPs were thus well-placed to build a strong focus of ethnicity into their local work. That most of them did not do so represented a very serious policy and practice failure.

Poverty and deprivation amongst BME children: the implications for Sure Start

The UK's BME groups as a whole are more likely to be in poverty than the population at large (Craig, 1999, 2002; Palmer et al., 2004; Platt, 2003, 2007; Flaherty et al., 2004). Research indicates that the UK's ethnic minorities are marked as much by diversity and difference, within and between particular minority groups, as by their common experience of racism (both individual and institutional) and discrimination. A wide range of welfare outcomes are poor for most minorities, although there are differences also between (and sometimes within) minority groups. Class and gender divisions can also create significant differences within specific minority groups.

This link between poverty and minority ethnic status reflects high unemployment levels, racism and discrimination in the selection of people for jobs or redundancy, greater likelihood of being in low-paid work; difficulties in accessing welfare services, including benefits; and restrictions on state financial help for refugees and asylum-seekers. The ways these factors have played out in recent years in terms of access to the labour market have been demonstrated both by large-scale investigations (for example, Cabinet Office, 2003) and by smaller-scale qualitative studies (for example, Craig et al., 2005). Poor outcomes for minorities have been observed in terms of poverty (Craig, 1999, 2004; Platt, 2007), health (Nazroo, 2001; Blofeld, 2004; Salway et al., 2007), labour market participation (Cabinet Office, 2003; Craig et al., 2005; Clark and Drinkwater, 2007), education (SEU, 1998; Gilborn and Mirza, 2000; Craig, 2005; Bagguley and Hussain, 2007), housing (Law, 2003), the criminal justice system (Cole et al., 2006), and in relation to the welfare system as a whole (Parekh, 2000).

Levels of poverty amongst children of minority ethnic origin were highlighted by the Greater London Authority (GLA, 2003). This research showed that Bangladeshi and Pakistani households together had the highest percentage of children living in income poverty (73 per cent), and that half of all Black children were living in income poverty. It is worth observing that a detailed analysis is still not possible in many policy and geographical areas because of the lack of adequate data – particularly in areas with relatively small minority populations (see Darr et al., 2004; McKendrick et al., 2007) – and much of what we know still relies on relatively small-scale qualitative research (Craig, 2005).

There is also limited data available from national surveys. The large-scale survey and secondary analysis of other data sets undertaken by Gordon (2000) concluded that, in relation to a basket of socially-defined necessities, the proportion of children living in families lacking one or more items was, for example, almost twice as high for 'non-white' families as it was for white families. Large numbers of children within families have been associated historically with a greater risk of poverty: the Health Survey of England tells us that 47 per cent and 43 per cent respectively of Bangladeshi and Pakistani households had three or more children compared with 16 per cent for both white and African-Caribbean populations (DoH, 2000). Modood et al. (1997) put the gap between these groupings as even larger.

It is important to remember, however, that about 40 per cent of the UK's ethnic minority population was actually born in the UK, and this results in important differences of an inter-generational kind (Atkin et al., 2001), with differing attitudes, norms and dress, and educational, social and economic expectations. These differences may translate at a local level into differing expectations and use of Sure Start programmes between different minority groups, dependent in part on length of settlement in this country as well as on cultural norms.

In general terms, people of Chinese and Indian origin tend to do better than the average (and often better than the white UK population) in terms of economic and educational achievement, those of Bangladeshi and Pakistani rather worse than average, with people of black African and African-Caribbean origin exhibiting a less clear-cut pattern. Within what are commonly regarded as single ethnic groupings, there may be marked differences; for example, research on the UK's Turkish population shows how there is a hierarchy between the three groupings of mainland Turks, Cypriot Turks and Kurdish Turks in terms of educational attainment (Enneli et al., 2005). A focus on ethnicity must therefore incorporate a strong sense of difference and diversity, which is reflected also in different forms of household structure (JCLR, 2000), child-rearing practices, and differing levels and forms of labour market participation, all factors relevant to the goals of Sure Start. SSLPs in multicultural areas therefore faced a challenging task to orient services sensitively to these various norms and expectations within an overall context of deprivation.

There is also a potential impact of gender differences on engagement with SSLPs. Women of African-Caribbean origin have relatively high labour market participation rates, with implications for childcare issues. Barely a quarter of African-Caribbean respondents to Middleton and Ashworth's survey of children's lifestyles (1995) were able to use grand-parents to provide childcare (compared with about 70 per cent of South Asian families and 50 per cent of white families). This has impacts on disposable income for these families. Many spend a substantial propor-tion of their income on childcare. Modood et al. (1997) also found that African-Caribbean women not only had the lowest level of free childcare and used childminders relatively more than any other ethnic group, but that those using childcare paid for all or some of their childcare at a rate (58 per cent) almost twice that of the next highest scoring group. The Social Exclusion Unit has noted that children from minority back-grounds are less likely to access childcare and nurseries (SEU, 2004). Consultation by the DayCare Trust with minority parents found again that childcare services were 'insensitive to the differing needs and per-ceptions of ethnic (sic) communities' (Stubbs, 2003: 6), with some par-ents reporting outright racism in service delivery. The DayCare Trust (2006) reported that BME families face substantial barriers to childcare, including cost, lack of flexibility and access to information. Strikingly, given the myth that South Asian families 'look after their own', the Health Survey for England (DoH, 2000) found that substantially greater proportions of Indian, Pakistani, Bangladeshi and Chinese families reported a more severe lack of support than was the case with English and African-Caribbean populations.

Because organisations do not monitor data effectively, and even large-scale surveys fail adequately to capture the dimension of ethnicity, there was a need for a strong dimension of ethnicity within NESS, within national and regional guidance from the Department for Education and Skills, regional government offices, and within local planning and pol-icy documents. A strong focus on ethnicity in the national programme would have ensured that SSLPs targeted their work on local minorities and would also have offered the opportunity to address the data deficit, but the data collated nationally by NESS did not adequately capture diversity, and local data collection has been patchy and inconsistent. Only a very limited number of local evaluations commented on the dimension of ethnicity (see also Lloyd and Rafferty, 2006), and there was no requirement that local evaluations should look at the 'ethnic dimension'. The categories of ethnicity used by NESS – typically Asian, black and white – were too broad to capture the experience of diverse minorities within most SSLPs.

Although the choice of SSLP areas had resulted in the inclusion of an over-representation of areas with relatively high proportions of minority ethnic families, neither NESS's research interventions, nor documentation from the Sure Start Unit at the DfES, addressed the dimension of ethnicity to an adequate extent; and neither the Sure Start Unit nor government regional offices monitored the extent to which the guidance about engaging with minorities was followed in practice. Even where information about ethnicity was collected, there were critical areas (such as the voluntary involvement of parents, the specific roles of minority staff, and ethnic monitoring at all levels in the organisation) where data on the performance of SSLPs was not available. This was the context within which we reviewed the practice of 12 SSLPs.

Working in areas of ethnic diversity

All 12 case study SSLPs examined, chosen to reflect a range of local demographic contexts, had been established for long enough to fully address issues of ethnicity in their work. Most were in areas of high deprivation and considerable ethnic diversity, but we also chose several study areas with small minority populations, either to see how work was targeted on BME communities in these areas or to look at work with specific minority populations, in particular traveller populations. The proportion of the populations from BME communities in the studies ranged from about 2 per cent to over 70 per cent.

This chapter highlights major issues identified from our study. While there were significant deficiencies in the programme at national, regional and local levels, there were examples of good practice, some of which we cite as boxed examples. These were the exception rather than the rule. The best attempts at involving BME communities occurred when they were sustained and structurally integrated into the work of the SSLP.

Promoting diverse images

Presenting positive images of minorities was an important way both of stressing the commitment of the SSLP to diversity and ensuring that the programme was not dominated by one minority group. Programmes used a variety of posters, pictures and publicity material, celebrated important festivals and generally paid attention to different cultural signifiers such as dress and food requirements. This was an important way in which the SSLP environment was able to promote and enhance a multicultural approach.

A strategic approach to working in areas of ethnic diversity requires:

- gathering effective monitoring data;
- analysing data appropriately, constantly updating it to inform new services;
- promoting effective community-based consultation, making contact with specific minority communities in ways congruent with their community life (including use of their meeting places);
- developing mainstream services which were accessible equally to all minority communities;
- using a range of publicity material (not just written material) to make contact;
- developing targeted outreach work;
- sensitising other local projects and programmes to work with minorities;
- employing a range of staff from different local minorities, offering effective opportunities for advancement;
- providing comprehensive translation and interpretation services;
- working to overcome critical cultural and religious barriers;
- consciously working across ethnic boundaries.

Often SSLP staff in positions of leadership were not making best use of available knowledge about working with BME groups or sharing information with less experienced staff. Thus, data collected by the SSLPs rarely paid attention to BME communities or their needs. Conducted effectively, with a focus on the dimension of ethnicity *inter alia*, local evaluations, which also in a structured way built on the views of local parents, could be powerful tools for promoting organisational change and community responsiveness. Most, however, failed to do this.

The issue of working with minorities had to be given priority throughout the SSLP's life. This did not happen where there were competing priorities or where there was a cost issue involved. Delivering services to minorities can have cost implications because of the need for a longer lead-in time, greater levels of development work, the cost of interpretation and translation, and so on. Recognition of these additional costs requires a strategic appraisal of the levels of resource available to children's centres – so that those with significant and diverse minority populations are better resourced.

Thinking about the practice of SSLPs

The questions which should be asked in order to refocus services to make them accessible to minorities include: 'Is this service universal?', 'Is it equally accessible to all?', 'Are there specific services which identified minorities might need?', 'Are additional barriers to accessing services faced by certain minorities?'

Few SSLPs had rigorously applied such questioning to their strategic approach, to thinking about operational details and day-to-day practice, or in monitoring and reviewing their work from time to time. Local minorities' experiences and perceptions – potentially important sources of local data for shaping service development – were drawn on relatively infrequently.

The upside and downside of parental involvement

Some SSLPs had tried to involve parents in the structure and development of the SSLP, training them in aspects of its work; for example, to undertake evaluative work or as interpreters to work with other parents. One SSLP trained a number of parents, but unfortunately – at least for SSLP staff – most had then gained paid employment (which might be regarded as a positive outcome for them) and the scheme had not been repeated. In another area, there had been several attempts to have a minority parent chair the management committee (partnership board). However, none of the other members of the board were BME members, leaving the chair quite isolated.

Parental involvement is critical to the future of such work. It provides a vehicle for community capacity-building as well as supporting the changing aspirations of parents, for example, allowing women to venture beyond traditional roles.

In several SSLPs, staff talked about simply providing services on 'an equal basis' without recognising that there were barriers – of knowledge, information, culture, religion, suspicion, fear – which might hinder some BME communities from accessing services. This is an area where stronger central guidance from the Sure Start Unit as to what 'equal opportunity' means, in reality, would have helped.

The appointment of minority staff workers and advisers in a variety of roles was an important step for some programmes. However, this could allow the SSLP in question to neglect race awareness work for other staff. Work with minorities can become ghettoised, so that minorities alone think about race awareness issues, and the whole staff team are not required to address the issues involved. In many areas SSLP staff noted that there had been no general attempt to incorporate race awareness work on an ongoing basis for all staff. This seems a remarkable lacuna given the terms of the Race Relations Amendment Act 2000 and government sponsorship of Sure Start. This omission should not be repeated in children's centres.

Where minority staff worked in programmes at a senior level and influenced the overall direction of the SSLP, this provided both an actual and a symbolic benefit.

Appointing local community staff: costs and benefits

The case for appointing staff from the local community was put enthusiastically by one programme manager: 'If you come from that culture, you have a lot more idea of what is going on. We can only try and understand, we haven't got the inner workings ... some of them needed skills, we have really, really developed [them] ...' In this programme, early team members had not been recruited from the local community. Although it took a year, local recruitment had eventually been successful. This meant that the team was culturally attuned to the needs of the whole community. White team members felt they could rely on Asian staff members for guidance when they needed it. Many SSLPs reported that the use of BME staff as role models was very positive, especially in the delivery of specific services such as outreach or in providing the first point of contact for new users. In one area, however, Asian workers felt that cultural diversity training was too basic and might lead to cultural stereotyping.

Although the appointment of minority staff was symbolically important in terms of the general orientation of SSLPs, consequent difficulties could occur. One SSLP, in a very diverse multicultural area, had had about half of its early staff from ethnic minorities. However, as staff left, those that replaced them, including all of the senior management team, were white. In this, and other SSLPs, staff and parents were disturbed by the shift away from a strong minority presence.

Managing a staff team response to diversity

In an inner city area, the SSLP and many of its partner organisations were effectively run by members of BME groups. In one early years team, staff spoke up to 12 different languages. In several other SSLPs, a generally welcoming atmosphere, regardless of culture or ethnicity, was commented on by parents. Ethnic matching was also important in relation to the use of parents as volunteers. One programme had initiated story-telling by South Asian story-tellers for parents and children. Another had used trained volunteers for interpretation and translation where minority numbers were small.

Another specific area where there was insufficient guidance from government was in the general area of community cohesion, an issue which has now achieved high policy salience. Given that residential segregation was marked in some of the case study areas, programmes like Sure Start presented ideal opportunities for promoting cross-ethnic links and interaction. Despite good work by specific SSLPs, this opportunity for thinking through the issues was not widely recognised and used.

Building bridges

Minority communities, including a traveller community, were drawn into the work of the SSLP through a cooking activity. Travellers had requested something to do with cooking, and staff felt this could provide a good opportunity to build bridges between different sections of the community. A traveller mother had been harassed by her 'giorgio' (non-traveller) neighbours, but at a mixed session at the SSLP she felt that 'nobody judges me here for my culture'. In another SSLP, the idea of an 'edible quilt' had emerged where one group cooked healthy food for parents from other national or ethnic origins and then one of the other groups would reciprocate. Some programmes took advantage of high-profile events, such as the Asian tsunami, to bring groups together for celebration or commemoration.

SSLPs needed more help on *how* engagement with minority communities might happen, and appropriate forms of support, including training, to encourage this. Such support needed to ensure that stated overall goals and legislative requirements in relation to involvement of ethnic minorities specifically, and promotion of equal opportunities more broadly, were adhered to at local level. Some SSLP staff had relevant expertise but many more did not and were effectively left in isolation to develop approaches to working with minorities. Since there was a substantial body of knowledge available, including within some SSLPs, this was a wasted opportunity.

Overall, then, the failure of the Sure Start programme as a whole centrally to approach the issue of working with BME communities led to important local consequences. Data on ethnic communities and experience of working with them was not gathered adequately by national or local evaluations. Social and economic indicators suggested that the programme, though universal in the areas in which it operated, should be strongly targeted on minority communities. This happened in some places, but insufficiently to allow this very heavy investment in local programmes to provide invaluable evidence about best practice in working with minority communities. Despite many interesting and important areas of work, the National Sure Start programme – and its associated National Evaluation – represents a major missed opportunity for enhancing the lives of marginalised minority communities. This may be even more the case for those groups typically described as 'hard to reach', particularly those of traveller/Roma origin, migrant workers, or certain more 'mainstream' BME groups such as those of Bangladeshi origin.

Key messages

In conclusion, there is a number of issues which emerging children's centres should address if they are to take the issue of delivering services to and engaging with minority communities effectively. This agenda is made more urgent in light of the National Audit Office (2006) report, which noted that fewer than one-third of the government's flagship children's centres were reaching out to the neediest families they were meant to target.

- Children's centres should take a wide **community development role** engaging with local community organisations and encouraging them to work with centres. This is not necessarily the same as outreach work.
- **Targeted services** are central in reaching minorities effectively. The 'colour-blind' approach to service delivery has been discredited in most 'race'-oriented service and policy. Centres need very strong central guidance on understanding difference and diversity, and their implications for service delivery.
- We also emphasise the importance of **outreach work**: varied, appropriate and linked to the targeting approach described above.

Using volunteers to promote outreach

SSLPs used parents as volunteers to help with outreach work. In some areas peer group members encouraged new minority group parents to use SSLPs. Others had used parents as informal interpreters of publicity material within their own communities. Yet others had acted as informal reception staff to welcome casual callers.

- Very uneven use was made of **translation and interpretation** work. In some areas it was comprehensive and effective. In others it exhibited many examples of poor practice, including the use of relatives, inappropriate use of peer group members, or little or no use of translation at all. Key issues here are not just about the importance of the service but who should undertake it.
- Many SSLPs needed to review their **employment practices**, and children's centres will need to do the same. Very few minority staff were employed in senior roles which had important symbolic effects within and outside programmes. In-service training, support and mentoring are needed for minority staff to take advantage of opportunities for advancement and promotion on equal terms with their colleagues. The same general considerations apply to the use of parent volunteers.
- The strategic approach of children's centres should be based on a continual **renewal of services**; not only are new residents becoming parents but new

groups are moving into areas. Demographic change is moving more rapidly than ever before in Sure Start areas, and centres will need to re-evaluate their services annually.

- The impact of **national and regional guidance** was uneven at best, non-existent at worst, adding to the picture of considerable variation at local level. It is appropriate to stress the importance of local centres reflecting local needs in their working methods, but this is not the same thing as ignoring the wide range of good practice available from other sources for helping programmes work in often complex and difficult areas. There is no necessary tension between strong central guidance and local autonomy and responsiveness.

- It is important to be able to **analyse** how **outcomes** for varying minority groups vary from the local children's population as a whole. This will depend on better monitoring data and the use of sensitive and appropriate ethnic categorisation.

- It is essential to recognise the growing issues **around difference and diversity within and between minority groups.** Working with particular groups has to be tailored very closely to the particular religious and cultural context within which services are operating. What works in one area does not necessarily work in others; for example, in building links with particular ethnic communities or working with men. Additionally, working with some communities takes much longer – because of issues of religion, culture, language, mistrust, local history, conflict and so on – and this has implications for resourcing work.

- Finally, we emphasise the role that programmes such as Sure Start – and hence children's centres – can play in promoting **community cohesion,** building mutual trust and respect between different communities. There was some limited evidence of this happening through bridge-building activities. Much more might have been done and at a time when Islamophobia and racist attacks on both Muslims and others are increasing as a result of tensions generated by terrorist attacks and the so-called 'war on terror', the opportunities for bringing different minorities together and with the majority population within a safe context of shared interests is an important one.

Note

1 Gary Craig is Professor of Social Justice at the University of Hull. He led a team of researchers which explored the dimension of ethnicity in the Sure Start national programme. The full report of this study is available at www.dfes.gov.uk/research (or from G.Craig@hull.ac.uk). Other members of the research team were Sue Adamson, Nasreen Ali, Shehzad Ali, Lynn Atkins, Abena Dadze-Arthur, Charmaine Elliott, Sara McNamee and Bano Murtuja.

References

Atkin, K., Ahmad, W.I.U. and Jones, L. (2001) 'Young South Asian deaf people and their families: negotiating relationships and identities', *Sociology of Health and Illness*, 24(1): 21–45.

Bagguley, P. and Hussain, Y. (2007) *The Role of Higher Education in Providing Opportunities for South Asian Women*. Bristol: Policy Press.

Blofeld, J., Sir (2004) *Report on Enquiry into Death of Michael Bennett*. London: Department of Health.

Cabinet Office (2003) *Ethnic Minorities and the Labour Market*. London: Cabinet Office Strategy Unit.

Clark, K. and Drinkwater, S. (2007) *Ethnic Minorities in the Labour Market*. Bristol: Policy Press.

Cole, B., Davidson, N., Adamson, S., Murtuja, B. and Craig, G. (2006) *Trust in the Law?* Leeds: West Yorkshire Criminal Justice Board.

Craig, G. (1999) '"Race", poverty and social security', in J. Ditch (ed.), *Introduction to Social Security*. London: Routledge.

Craig, G. (2002) 'Welfare, citizenship and racism: a European perspective', in J-G. Andersen and P. Jensen (eds), *Welfare, Citizenship and the Labour Market*. Bristol: Policy Press.

Craig, G. (2004) 'Citizenship, exclusion and older people', *Journal of Social Policy*, 30(1): 95–114.

Craig, G. (2005) 'Black and minority ethnic children', in G. Preston (ed.), *At Greatest Risk?* London: Child Poverty Action Group.

Craig, G. (2007) 'Cunning, loathsome and despicable: the racist tail wags the welfare dog', *Journal of Social Policy*, 36(4): 605–624.

Craig, G., Dietrich, H. and Gautie, J. (2005) 'Excluded youth or young citizens?: ethnicity, young people and the labour market in three EU countries', in J. Hoof and H. Bradley (eds), *Young People, Labour Markets and Social Citizenship*. Bristol: Policy Press.

Darr, A., Atkin, K. and Craig, G. (2004) *Ethnic Minorities in a Rural Labour Market*. York: North Yorkshire Learning and Skills Council and Universities of Hull and Leeds.

DayCare Trust (2006) *Ensuring Equality: Black and Minority Ethnic Families' Views on Childcare*. London: DayCare Trust.

DoH (2000) *Health Survey of England*. London: Department of Health.

Enneli, P., Bradley, H. and Modood, T. (2005) *Turks and Kurds*. Bristol: Policy Press.

Flaherty, J., Veit-Wilson, J. and Dornan, P. (2004) *Poverty: The Facts*, 5th edition. London: Child Poverty Action Group.

Gilborn, D. and Mirza, H. (2000) *Educational Inequality: Mapping Race, Class and Gender*. London: Institute of Education.

GLA (2003) *London Divided*. London: Greater London Authority.

Gordon, D. (2000) *Poverty and Social Exclusion in Britain*. York: Joseph Rowntree Foundation.

JCLR (2000) *National Child Development Study 2000 and 1970: British Cohort Study Follow-Ups*. London: Joint Centre for Longitudinal Research, University of London.

Law, I. (2003) *Racism, Ethnicity and Social Policy*, 2nd edition. Hemel Hempstead: Harvester Wheatsheaf.

Lloyd, N. and Rafferty, A. (2006) *Black and Minority Ethnic Families and Sure Start: Findings from Local Evaluation Reports*. London: National Evaluation of Sure Start.

McKendrick, J., Mooney, G., Dickie, J. and Kelly, P. (eds) (2007) *Poverty in Scotland*. London: Child Poverty Action Group/Poverty Alliance.

Middleton, S. and Ashworth, K. (1995) *Small Fortunes: National Survey of the Lifestyles and Living Standards of Children*. Loughborough: CRSP, University of Loughborough.

Modood, T., Berthoud, R., Lakey, J., Nazroo, J., Smith, P., Virdee, S. and Beishon, S. (1997) *Ethnic Minorities in Britain*. London: Policy Studies Institute.

National Audit Office (2006) *Sure Start Children's Centres* (HC104 Session 2006–2007). London: HMSO.

Nazroo, J. (2001) *Ethnicity, Class and Health*. London: Policy Studies Institute.

Palmer, G., North, J., Carr, J. and Kenway, P. (2003) *Monitoring Poverty and Social Exclusion*. London: New Policy Institute.

Parekh, B. (Chair) (2000) *The Future of Multi-ethnic Britain*. London: Runnymede Trust.

Platt, L. (2003) *Parallel Lives?* London: Child Poverty Action Group.

Platt, L. (2007) *Poverty and Ethnicity in the UK*. York: Joseph Rowntree Foundation.

Salway, S., Platt, L., Chowbey, L., Harriss, K. and Bayliss, E. (2007) *Long-term Ill-health, Poverty and Ethnicity*. Bristol: Policy Press.

SEU (1998) *Truancy and School Exclusion*. London: Social Exclusion Unit, Cabinet Office.

SEU (2004) *Tackling Social Exclusion*. London: Social Exclusion Unit, Cabinet Office.

Stubbs, S. (2003) 'Childcare needs an ethnic mix', *Community Care*, 17 October: 6.

5 Empowering Parents

Fiona Williams

This chapter:

- discusses what is meant by empowerment
- explores the extent to which Sure Start Local Programmes (SSLPs) empowered people as parents and community members
- identifies routes parents followed to gain a stronger sense of self and self-determination
- draws out lessons learned for the ways professionals understand and engage with service users.

Key questions:

o What does parental empowerment mean and why is it important?
o How can professionals promote empowerment for service users and providers?
o How did SSLPs improve some parents' perceptions of their roles and responsibilities?
o What are the implications for the way children's centres respond to their local communities?

A Sure Start goal was to empower parents by giving them access to parenting support, enabling them to become active service-users and more confident parents. The importance of the parental empowerment approach lay in its positive implications for parent–child relations and the well-being of children (Pugh et al., 1994). SSLPs were encouraged to deliver services in a responsive and inclusive way, and to challenge negative perceptions about the local communities they served. Engaging with parents was seen as a way of combating social exclusion by developing community cohesion. Such an approach marked a significant break with past professional practices, which were characterised by a more individualised, hierarchical, formal and expert approach to the relationship with users (Williams, 1999). The lessons of this intervention, then, are important for an understanding of the possibilities for the future social relations of family support services generally, not only those for parents and young children.

What is meant by empowerment?

In general terms empowerment means a shift from a state of vulnerability or lack of power to enhanced power or control. However, the implications for social intervention can be different according to whether the focus is on the individual, on institutions and professional practices, or on the wider community and cultural, social and structural factors.

Individual empowerment

Individual empowerment refers to personal development of, say, self-esteem, confidence or feelings of self-worth that have been shaped or damaged by experiences of poverty, stigma or emotional deprivation. Empowerment for parents might involve personal development in the form of new awareness of their own strengths, assets, skills and resources to enhance their lives.

Another form of personal empowerment refers to the notion of 'voice', that is, having a say in local service provision. At the individual level, this tends to be restricted to the possibility of encouraging people to become 'consumers' of services, to be aware of their choices, to exercise their choice according to their needs, and to have the possibility to voice dissatisfactions (Starkey, 2003).

On their own, these individual approaches to empowerment have their limitations. Experiences of disempowerment may have less to do with lack of personal attributes and more to do with continued lack of resources or forms of disadvantage such as unemployment, poor housing or pervasive racism. Increased self-esteem can enable someone to only manage these effects rather than minimize them. Similarly, while having a say in service delivery and being able to look elsewhere for better services is a vital component of empowerment, it is often the most articulate and assertive who tend to have their voices heard and who have the real power to search out good services (Taylor et al., 1992).

Even so, giving someone the confidence to act in purposive, autonomous and creative ways is important. In academic literature this capacity to act has been referred to as people's 'agency' (Williams et al., 1999; Hoggett, 2000). Although 'agency' is shaped by wider structural factors, it is not entirely determined by them. Furthermore, this sort of self-determination may be an important bridge to acting collectively with others in self-help groups, voluntary activities and campaigns. Having an awareness of agency is important to a person's identity and self-esteem, and is in turn influenced by them.

Lister (2004), for example, identifies four aspects of agency in the lives of people in poverty:

- 'getting by', which involves everyday coping strategies;
- 'getting back at' through day-to-day resistance to experiences of disrespect;
- strategies to 'get out' of poverty;
- strategies to 'get organised' and effect change.

Expressions of parental agency might therefore be found in everyday coping strategies; accessing, receiving and providing forms of care and support; advice, information, training, education, employment or enjoyment; individually or with others. What then becomes important is how far and in what ways professional practices enable or constrain these possibilities.

Institutions and practices that (dis)empower

Concerns about the disempowering effects of hierarchical professional practices emerged from many service-user movements, such as the women's health movement, the disability movement, and survivors' organizations, and has been central to the rethinking of how services should be delivered (Williams, 1999). Such practices include the bureaucratic and formal nature of professional working; use of unfamiliar jargon; lack of consultation; professionals 'know best' attitudes; and problematising particular social groups or family forms (Balloch and Taylor 2001; Ball 2002). These are especially relevant for parents in deprived areas.

A new approach to professional practice is concerned with how professionals impart their knowledge; how professional practices develop more equal, responsive, participatory and respectful relations; how they ascertain the needs and aspirations of parents who use services; how they are more inclusive and recognise the diversity of those needs; how they encourage parents into services and avoid inducing feelings of stigma; how they recognise the strengths that parents bring and not simply the problems they bear: in other words, how they enable parents' capacity for self-determination to flourish.

Social and community empowerment

The community development or 'liberationist' model of empowerment aims to challenge oppression, exclusion and power imbalances in society in a broader sense (Freire, 1972; Graham, 2002). This approach to empowerment recognises the way our social positioning impacts on our personal sense of power. A community or social change approach to empowerment will seek to tackle discrimination, inequality and disadvantage through awareness-raising, possibilities for collective action and community development. This might involve challenging perceptions about particular communities, raising issues of inadequate infrastructure – housing, unemployment – which can unite otherwise diverse communities, prioritising different groups' needs, or ensuring more grass-roots involvement in local and national decision making.

Key dynamics of parental empowerment

This chapter is based on a themed study which investigated parents' experiences of empowerment in six case study localities, to discover how and in what ways SSLPs were facilitating individual and community empowerment (Williams and Churchill, 2006).[1]

We developed a fourfold understanding of the key dynamics of parental empowerment operating at personal, group, institutional and community levels including:

- **Respect** – feeling valued as an individual, secure and not judged, having a sense of dignity, confidence and self-esteem for what and who you are; developing mutual respect.
- **Voice** – having the capacity and means to articulate one's needs, to participate and be listened to.
- **Self-determination** – having access to, and being able to make use of knowledge, skills, support, services, material and cultural resources in order to enhance the capacity to act and improve one's own and others' circumstances and opportunities.
- **Inclusive recognition** – feeling included, having a sense of belonging, having moral worth as a parent (and as a professional), a member of the community, and as a member of a social group, such as mother, father, lone parent, disabled parent, or member of minority ethnic or religious group.

We found substantial evidence of experiences of *individual* parent empowerment in all the case study areas, usually expressed by parents in terms of feeling less isolated, more valued (especially as mothers) and more listened to. They expressed more confidence in voicing their concerns and in their parenting. They reported feeling a closer bond with their children, who they felt were mixing more with other children and were better prepared for school. We found greater variation in the extent to which Sure Start had generated *group* and *community* empowerment, whether through mutual support amongst parents and other family members, parental involvement and volunteering and community-oriented actions. Key factors in the development of individual empowerment and more collectively community empowerment seemed to be the strength of programme ethos, how this interpreted empowerment in practice, and how its messages were communicated to the local community. In particular it was important for parents and volunteers to see this ethos in practice; and it was important that it *made sense* to the everyday experiences of parents, volunteers and staff. The development of a core of involved parents as 'community champions' who could mobilise others to get involved in activities at the grass-roots level was also important.

SSLP practices promoting empowerment

Practices promoting individual and community empowerment included:

- transforming professional relationships with parents;
- providing responsive and inclusive services;
- working with and developing communities and having a strong programme ethos.

Transforming professional relationships with parents

The style of programme delivery was influential in drawing parents into the services and determining whether they felt recognised and valued. Proficient SSLPs enhanced parents' trust, self-esteem and respect for themselves, service providers and other parents. Where parents felt valued and trusted, they were more likely to 'bond' and develop better mutual support systems.

Important aspects included:

Being welcoming, friendly, informal, facilitative and respectful, structured into the programme through a conscious development of 'welcoming behaviour' by staff – smiling, talking to parents, and introducing them to others. Buddying or befriending systems provided by parents to new parents were effective, particularly where befrienders shared a minority language. These approaches were highly valued by parents and made the difference between returning or not.

> 'It's like we're Sure Start, and it probably sounds really awful but we have our own little groups and we won't let anyone else in and that's starting to change now because we've got buddies, we've started a buddy scheme, so if we get a new parent coming in, a buddy will take them under their wing because a lot of the parents have been coming and then they haven't been coming back.' (Krista, parent)

Nevertheless, informality created its own problems, leaving programmes open to accusations of favouritism and had to be balanced by a conscious strategy of inclusiveness.

Being supportive and non-judgmental, often described by parents and staff as engaging parents from 'where they are at'. One mother said she valued the way Sure Start staff got to know her situation, and compared this with her relationship with her health visitor from the hospital who, she felt, was more judgmental and 'didn't get to know your circumstances'. This ethos had an important multiplier effect on parent volunteers, as Farah, a parent volunteer with other minority ethnic parents, explained:

> 'Well I never get at anybody else and what they're doing, whether it's right or wrong, I don't say "Oh that's wrong and you should do this or you should do that", I give them guidance, you know say if they, like my niece, if my sister-in-law gives her juice in a bottle, I say to her mum, "Using a cup is better because you're giving her motor skills and she's being more independent and causing less sugar on her teeth", you get round it as well, and a lot of people, it's not that they don't care, it's not that they're being ignorant, it's just that they don't know that it causes problems, it's making them aware.'

Many parents said Sure Start staff were 'more like a friend', but they would turn to staff to discuss problems rather than to friends, because they felt more secure in SSLP staff's commitment to confidentiality.

Valuing parents' own experience and knowledge provided a good basis for encouraging parental involvement (such as in breast-feeding peer counselling) and the development of employability skills. A personal development approach encouraged reflexivity about being a parent through courses and parent groups, and avoided blaming or shaming. In a number of areas the skills parents brought with them were harnessed to provide support for others (for example, sports coaching).

Encouraging parents to 'voice' their needs provided a basis for consultation and for responsive and participative services. Encouraging parents to define their own problems provided opportunities for discussion and dialogue about different needs, and opened up choices, disagreements and strategies to parents. Talking about community needs reinforced a sense of common identity and belonging, and dialogue of this kind put staff priorities into perspective.

Providing responsive and accessible services

SSLPs' provision of responsive, accessible, available, flexible and inclusive services enhanced parents' access to resources and gave them greater capacity for self-determination. This could involve:

- providing services and activities at a number of local sites;
- providing a transport service for those with mobility constraints;

- taking services to people in their homes;
- communicating to parents through regular outreach about services and opportunities;
- telephone contact to inform parents about new opportunities and services;
- information, such as a newsletters and leaflets to every household;
- free or low-cost provision;
- information translated orally or as texts for minority languages, use of pictures in advertising;
- parent befriending schemes.

Dedicated outreach work reinforced the universal nature of services. It militated against perceptions of unfairness or cliquey-ness, or that services were meant only for one particular social or ethnic group. It involved parents (and staff) in ways that developed their own communication skills, and community identity. It provided information to ensure responsive services and facilitated preventative work, especially in relation to family support and health. It helped break down perceptions of staff as institutionalised or distant. Regular outreach and home-based services ensured that those with mobility problems, due to health or domestic demands, could access services. Volunteering and the development of mutual support systems provided opportunities for parents to meet and learn from new parents and to develop alliances and create 'bridges' across social groups. Meeting other people, as one parent put it, 'opens your mind'.

The chair of a local Bangladeshi welfare organisation explained the cultural and domestic constraints of Bangladeshi women in accessing services: 'You have to go out to them. You have to meet them where they are at, to empower them, you need to meet them, in their houses ... They live very local lives.' (Mrs C)

Mothers often became friends and exchanged babysitting and childcare. Some programmes set up groups that became mutually supportive and autonomous: a parents' group that became a constituted parents' action group, a young parents' group, a community action group, an Arabic women's group, and a group for parents with children with a particular disability. Groups were based on common experience of parents, particular interests, or specific circumstances that parents faced. They sometimes managed to bring harder-to-reach parents, such as fathers, into their orbit. Some programmes created stepping stones for parents to take up training that would equip them to become volunteers, and then lead them into employment. Some volunteers became active 'community champions'.

Working with communities: strong ethos and sensitivity to context

Group and community empowerment depended on three dimensions: a robust programme ethos; connecting this ethos to the local context; having a positive approach to the local community and being able to create a community presence. The scope given to SSLPs to design their own programmes gave rise in a number of areas to a strong programme ethos exemplified in the priorities and actions of staff, and the degree to which there was a shared sense of purpose generated by mutual dialogue across the staff (and parent) team, particularly between team leaders, programme managers and front-line staff. It often emerged from the commitment of a programme manager or management team who had a vision of different ways of delivering services, transforming the provider/user relationship, having a holistic and preventative approach to problem-solving, an interdisciplinary approach to professional expertise, and a constructive approach to the capacities of parents and communities. It was important that such an ethos connected with parents, volunteers and staff and made sense to them. Where it did, trust, reciprocity and greater capacity for individual and community self-determination followed, and staff morale was high. A strong ethos also led to programmes being prepared to go outside the central government Sure Start remit and be less 'target driven'.

A strong ethos was more likely to be sensitive to, and able to work with, cultural differences. Often ethnic diversity in a programme area created particular challenges, not because of any intrinsic 'problem' with multi-ethnic groups, but because of practical and historical issues that created further complexities and costs to strategies and priorities (see Chapter 4 for a detailed discussion). Sure Start teams which were strongly embedded in and identified with the local community, and had staff with community development backgrounds, were better placed and were less likely to stereotype the characteristics of minority ethnic groups. Questions of ethnicity were also relevant to the mainly white programme areas.

Key messages: parental empowerment

Drawing on parents' experiences of SSLPs, we identified seven interconnected routes to empowerment building on Lister's four dimensions of agency in the lives of people in poverty.

Individual empowerment

Getting by refers to a sense of coping and surviving on a day-by-day basis, with the support and resources drawn from involvement with their SSLP. Some parents were helped to overcome a crisis, such as drug addiction, unemployment, mental illness or bereavement, whilst others received more informal and professional support to cope, and to feel more positive about everyday life. Kelvin describes reaching a new understanding about himself and his parenting through the reception of practical, non-judgemental and reassuring support:

> 'Sure Start gave me that kick. They stressed to me about what my kids needed. They didn't need a drugged-up dad, they needed a role model … I spend time with the kids now. I believe in myself a bit more now. I think more about the children's welfare, we have more respect for one another as a family. The children are going to school now, they didn't before.'

In many cases, providing support for families on the brink of a crisis was the consequence of dedicated, ongoing, outreach work.

Getting better at everyday living involved gaining confidence and self-respect and becoming more capable. Issues of self-perception and self-identity were common themes in parents' discussions, and parents gained confidence by receiving reassurance and encouragement from other parents and staff members. Being able not just to receive help and support but also to help others was a very important source of feeling more capable and positive.

Getting on was when parents started to develop new skills in order to realise their aspirations, often but not always in paid work, and to become more self-determining. They felt their children were happy and flourishing, and they respected them more:

> 'I think as a mother, I learnt quite a lot of new things, how to go with them, how to communicate with them, how to keep your temper when you're feeling quite angry you know, not just clashing and banging there and I think, and respecting them more.' (Karam, parent)

Getting out: while some parents had gained the confidence and skills to want to put these back into the community, others had aspirations to move out of their area, in order to seek better paid work, school or housing opportunities. Sometimes, those who had become champions for their community through volunteering left to go to community development jobs elsewhere.

Community empowerment

Getting together often brought parents into contact with people from different backgrounds. It could lead to a change in parents' perceptions of their neighbours and fellow residents. Parents commented that their horizons had been broadened by Sure Start.

Getting involved in organising, planning and designing Sure Start activities led to many empowering outcomes, such as parents being more confident about voicing their ideas. For some of the more involved parents, being more informed of local services and opportunities led them to become more involved in informing others.

Getting organised to improve the local environment through collective clean ups, to raise funding to improve local safety for children, brought people together in ways that could unite and give communities greater collective confidence, and build up those communities. In one area, for example, the setting up of a breast-feeding group led to successful campaigning for more facilities for breast-feeding mothers in the locality. Being involved in such groups, often facilitated initially by staff, meant that parents gained important skills in income generation and knowledge of community resources and democratic processes.

In the dimensions of empowerment we outlined earlier in the chapter – respect, voice, self-determination and inclusive recognition – Sure Start made a difference to parents. Feeling respected and respecting others, having greater individual, and sometimes collective, voice to articulate needs and, in some cases, to pressure for change, developing greater self-determination to use resources and access services in the ways they felt fit. This could enhance a sense of belonging and inclusion in local communities.

Key messages

The positive picture of empowerment gained from the study was not without problems and tensions. Sometimes parents felt that too much was expected of them or that Sure Start raised aspirations which could not be met. They felt that young people were more in need of resources and support than under-fours. Sometimes SSLP workers did not fully appreciate the implications of parents' lack of language and literacy skills. Some parents felt labelled as 'needy' or 'deprived', and others that parents who had got involved became 'cliquey'. Barriers to accessing services – timing, location, transport, mobility, waiting lists, costs and domestic demands – were considerable. There was sometimes a tension between informal relationships between staff and users, and the need for staff to be objectively impartial in their work. There were difficulties in engaging with fathers as a group rather than at individual levels. This inability to take the role of fathers seriously reflected a nationwide fault in welfare services (DfES/HM Treasury, 2007). Some parents who had worked with Sure Start found they could not gain equivalent work once they stepped outside the Sure Start community. Alternatively, training local people enabled them to leave the area, which then lost their skills. Programme managers were concerned that targets set nationally were not always the same as local needs or did not fit with local culture. For example, valuing women as mothers made them more self-confident as mothers, reinforcing their mothering as 'work'. This mitigated against fathers' involvement or mothers' wish to return to work. The geography of local programme areas led to those needing services beyond the catchment area being ineligible.

With the advent of children's centres, programme managers expressed concern about reduction of autonomy. Programme managers with clear vision had confidence to develop services in line with community needs. A particular success of Sure Start was its *multiplier effect*: the messages parents absorbed were passed on to other parents. Parents' relationships with each other, with their children and families, as well as with the community at large, were all influenced. Parents spoke about having been helped and 'wanting to give something back'. Processes of empowerment affected staff as much as parents and volunteers. The capacity to shape parents' confidence and self-determination depended upon *staff teams in SSLPs having the conditions to shape their own work and priorities.*

A second lesson concerns developing a new approach to professional working and engaging parents *across all professional disciplines and levels.* The approach places a premium on openness, accessibility, informality, non-judgementalism, listening, respecting and learning from parents' own experiences. This involves a recognition that respect begets respect between staff, parents, and their children, and creating a supportive environment which enables parents and communities to articulate their needs and to create respectful dialogues, especially when there are conflicting needs or perceptions of unfairness. A multidisciplinary approach, which uses community development skills together with the expertise of family support and health prevention work, is essential.

The 'ethic of care' (Williams, 2004), combined with a community empowerment approach, places a premium on sensitivity to context, on the articulation, communication and dialogue of needs as the basis to fairness, and on interdependence as the basis of human interaction. Applied to reconfigured children's services, the ethic stresses the importance of individuals pursuing different routes to empowerment and going at different paces. It requires creative and sensitive approaches to cultural and gender differences which do not blame or shame but foster diversity, community links, solidarity and belonging. It places importance on accessible and responsive services alongside outreach work to reach all parents. However, such an ethic creates a tension with those policies in education and social security which have put a premium on tests and targets and on children and parents as part of a 'social investment model' for society (Lister, 2003). While education and employment are important buffers to poverty, successful SSLPs framed their ethos in broader terms where education and skills enhanced emotional, physical, creative and democratic capabilities.

The importance of SSLPs was that they embodied, during a period when society was becoming diverse and heterogeneous, a universal approach to the enhancement of children's well-being, happiness and futures. The appeal engaged parents, creating new paths for improving participation and solidarity, but only when that engagement was rooted in the hopes, fears and desires that parents and their children articulated for themselves.

Note

1 I would like to thank Harriet Churchill who carried out most of the fieldwork, helped analyse the interviews, and contributed to the report; Bano Murtuja who interviewed some of the parents in their mother tongue; and Mog Ball for discussion of the findings. These were qualitative, in-depth and semi-structured interviews with parents (with different degrees of involvement in Sure Start), volunteers, staff and other local stakeholders in the six case-study areas. They were supplemented with participant and non-participant observation of groups, activities, meetings and events in the localities. We used purposive sampling methods to select the case studies and parent interviewees. The six areas were chosen to reflect urban and rural/high-to-low minority ethnic membership/high-to-low community activism/different local lead bodies/political contexts and history of SS funding. A total of 81 parents, 41 Sure Start staff and 38 stakeholders were interviewed. All names of people and places have been changed.

References

Ball, M. (2002) *Getting Sure Start Started*. London: NESS/DfES.

Balloch, S. and Taylor, M. (eds) (2001) *Partnership Working*. Bristol: Policy Press.

DfES/HM Treasury (Department for Education and Skills/Her Majesty's Treasury) (2007) 'The costs and benefits of active fatherhood', Paper prepared by Fathers' Direct to inform Joint Policy Review on Children and Young People. London: HMSO.

Freire, P. (1972) *Pedagogy of the Oppressed*. Harmondsworth: Penguin.

Graham, M. (2002) 'Creating spaces: exploring the role of cultural knowledge as a source of empowerment in models of social welfare in black communities', *British Journal of Social Work*, 32, 35–49.

Hoggett, P. (2000) *Emotional Life and the Politics of Welfare*. Basingstoke: Macmillan.

Lister, R. (2003) 'Investing in the citizen-workers of the future: transformations in citizenship and the state under New Labour', *Social Policy and Administration*, 37(5): 427–43.

Lister, R. (2004) *Poverty*. Basingstoke: Palgrave.

Pugh, G., De'Ath, E. and Smith, C. (1994) *Confident Parents, Confident Children: Policy and Practice in Parent Education and Support*. London: National Children's Bureau.

Starkey, F. (2003) 'The "empowerment debate": consumerist, professional and liberational perspectives in health and social care', *Social Policy and Society*, 2(4): 273–84.

Taylor, M., Hoyes, L., Lart, R. and Means, R. (1992) *User Empowerment in Community Care: Unravelling the Issues*. Bristol: Policy Press.

Williams, F. (1999) 'Good-enough principles for welfare', *Journal of Social Policy*, 28(4): 667–87.

Williams, F. (2004) *Rethinking Families*. London: Calouste Gulbenkian Foundation.

Williams, F. and Churchill, H. (2006) *Empowering Parents in Sure Start Programmes*. Research Report for the National Evaluation of Sure Start. London: DfES.

Williams, F., Popay, J. and Oakley, A. (1999) *Welfare Research: A Critical Review*. London: University College London Press.

Suggested further reading

Taylor, M., Hoyes, L., Lart, R. and Means, R. (1992) *User Empowerment in Community Care: Unravelling the Issues*. Bristol: Policy Press.

Williams, F. (2004) *Rethinking Families*. London: Calouste Gulbenkian Foundation.

Part 3

Children and Young People's Development

Supporting Transitions and Multi-agency Teamwork

The four chapters in this section are about delivering services. They focus on what practitioners do from day to day. Although the ethos of services needs to be welcoming, friendly and informal, the services themselves require rigour, clarity of purpose and adherence to provide evidence about what is effective. It is essential that quality is achieved and maintained in services and that staff operate at the highest levels of professionalism and integrity.

This happens when staff observe the rules and protocols of their own service, understand the impact of treatments on service users and also of the outcomes of treatments offered by partner professionals. It is incumbent on professional staff to keep up to date with evaluation evidence of good practice in their fields, and to share this with colleagues from other disciplines. They need to listen and learn from those colleagues in order to understand what may be available for families and when it might be appropriate to refer them for help. Good managers ensure that staff have the time and resources to make this happen.

There is no standard recipe of services for responding to family needs: families will want different ingredients, in different amounts and at different times. The practitioner needs systems to help them understand family needs – assessment frameworks, for example – and flexibility in responding directly or through referring users to other services. In family life there are multiple occasions of transition, from pregnancy to parenthood, from home care to day care, from day care to pre-school, and full-time parenting to training and employment. The multi-agency team responds with sensitivity, and with creativity as families progress. In order to do this the team must pay the closest attention to accurate, systematic monitoring of service use, its impact and cost/benefit.

Members of such teams need to think beyond the set routines of their own disciplines. Among the challenges they are liable to face are the competing demands of child and parent. Evidence tells us that confident parents make confident children, and that investment in support for parents will benefit the child. But ensuring that services ultimately benefit children requires constant attention. New ways of working can destabilise professional workers' sense of identity, and this can be painful. However, the gains are worth the pain: being part of a supportive professional community, learning from each other, and ultimately providing a better service.

6 Maternity Services

Jenny McLeish

This chapter:

- looks at policy and practice in maternity services
- discusses the remit for maternity services for Sure Start Local Programmes (SSLPs)
- reviews who delivered SSLP maternity services
- examines what the services looked like
- concludes with key lessons learned.

Key questions:

o What made SSLP maternity services different?

o What were the barriers SSLP health workers faced in innovating?

o How can inequalities in maternity service use be addressed and eliminated?

Policy and Practice

Maternity services are universal, but disadvantaged women are less likely to make optimum use of services and are at disproportionate risk of poor outcomes for both mother and baby, some of which may have life-threatening or life-long consequences. Groups at risk include young women, women whose first language is not English, homeless and travelling women, refugees and asylum seekers, women with problematic addiction to alcohol or drugs, and women experiencing domestic violence. At-risk groups were a focus for maternity services in SSLPs.

Maternity services are affected by two key drivers: on the one hand, a high-level policy commitment to improving services, especially for disadvantaged women, and on the other hand, a chronic shortage of midwives and health visitors to deliver those services. The Labour manifesto commitment in 2005, that every pregnant woman should have a choice of pain relief and have continuity of care from a known midwife, ensured that maternity services were high on the political agenda. This commitment was fleshed out in the publication of *Maternity Matters* (DoH, 2007).

Although *Maternity Matters* was framed in the language of choice, it recognised the significance of the maternity services as a public health intervention, and reminded commissioners and providers of the importance of meeting the needs of vulnerable and disadvantaged women and their partners. *Maternity Matters* built on a policy context that both influenced and was informed by the experience of providing maternity services in SSLPs.

Key initiatives in maternity services

The National Service Framework for Children, Young People and Maternity Services (NSF) (DoH and DfES, 2004: www.dh.gov.uk)   The maternity standard of the NSF, Standard 11, 'seeks to improve equity of access to maternity services, which will increase the survival rates and life chances for children from disadvantaged backgrounds.' It sets out a vision of 'flexible individualised services designed to fit around the woman and her baby's journey through pregnancy and motherhood, with emphasis on the needs of vulnerable and disadvantaged women'. It requires that 'maternity services are proactive in engaging all women, particularly women from disadvantaged groups and communities, early in their pregnancy and maintaining contact before and after birth.' It stresses the importance of co-ordinated multi-disciplinary and multi-agency partnerships ('managed maternity networks') to meet the needs of women with multiple social problems. It directs all National Health Service (NHS) maternity care providers and Primary Care Trusts (PCTs) to improve uptake of community maternity services and support for all pregnant women and new parents by 'extending Sure Start principles across other services' (DoH and DfES, 2004: 14).

National targets on maternity and inequality   The Department of Health's second Public Service Agreement (PSA) target is to reduce health inequalities by 10 per cent by 2010 as measured by infant mortality and life expectancy at birth (HM Treasury, 2004). The infant mortality target is supported by two targets for Local Delivery Plans:

- *Smoking:* deliver a 1 percentage point reduction per year in the proportion of women continuing to smoke throughout pregnancy, focusing especially on smokers from disadvantaged groups.
- *Breast-feeding:* deliver an increase of 2 percentage points per year in breast-feeding initiation rate, focusing especially on women in disadvantaged groups.

Guidance for maternity services commissioners from the Maternity Care Working Party (MCWP, 2006) underlined how high-quality maternity care can also contribute to meeting other PSA targets. These include reduction in adult and child mortality and tackling the underlying determinants of ill health (including smoking, childhood obesity and reducing the under-18 conception rate), as well as national strategies around mental health, diabetes, domestic abuse, substance misuse, HIV infections and parenting.

Clinical guidelines from the National Institute of Clinical and Health Excellence (NICE)   NICE issued evidence-based clinical guidelines on antenatal care in 2004, postnatal care in 2006, and antenatal and postnatal mental health in 2007 (see www.nice.org.uk).

The reorganisation of community midwifery to link with children's centres   Lessons from Sure Start were influential in the drive to make children's centres 'a focal point for the delivery of maternity services as part of a continuum of integrated services' (DfES, 2006: 53). However, in a repetition of early mistakes in some Sure Start local programmes, midwifery did not feature in the design of some children's centres, so that there was no space suitable for antenatal and postnatal clinics.

Staff shortages   Notwithstanding an increase in the workforce in recent years, maternity services in many areas report being overstretched and understaffed. In 2003, heads of midwifery (Curtis et al., 2003) identified their 'establishments' – the numbers of midwives who should be available in their units – as completely insufficient to meet the demands of the new policy imperatives. This situation was exacerbated by a combination of a rising birthrate (up from 54.7 births per thousand women aged 15–44 in 2001, to 58.4 per thousand in 2005), an aging workforce, and, most significantly, financial cuts in some trusts which led to posts being frozen or lost. In 2006, the Royal College of Midwives reported to the Select Committee on Health (House of Commons Health Committee, 2007) that more than one-third of managers surveyed stated that their maternity budget had been cut, more than a quarter that numbers of staff had been reduced (with half of these trusts operating a recruitment freeze), and that a quarter of senior midwives' posts were being replaced by junior posts. In some areas there were no longer enough midwives to conduct antenatal classes (Parkinson, 2007).

Health visitors were affected by similar trends, with fewer health visitors in the public health front line than at any time since 1994, 18 per cent of whom were over the retirement age of 55 (CPHVA/Amicus, 2006). A 2007 survey of 1,000 health visitors found that 55 per cent of them were making fewer visits to families because of increased caseloads, with the biggest impact being losing track of vulnerable families (CPHVA/Amicus, 2007).

What were SSLPS supposed to do?

SSLPs were required to provide enhanced maternity services: additional resources; improved access to services; new services to meet particular needs; new ways of working towards more effective delivery; collaboration with other services; and staff development and training. Targets included reduction in the incidence of low birth weight, reduction in the numbers of mothers smoking, increase in breast-feeding and improved hygiene and safety in the home. SSLPs had objectives for the culturally sensitive identification of, and support for, mothers experiencing postnatal depression, and support for parents to promote healthy child development before and after birth.

Some of the earliest SSLPs did little to improve mainstream NHS maternity services and in some cases had poor links with them, especially where maternity providers were not represented on the partnership board (see Chapter 2). But after new guidance was issued in 1999 (DfEE, 1999), SSLPs improved their proficiency in developing enhanced maternity services that targeted the risk factors or access issues identified in their local communities.

Who delivered the services?

Contractual arrangements

The most common arrangement was to fund a 'Sure Start midwife' or 'Sure Start health visitor' seconded from the mainstream services to provide an enhanced service to women and families in the SSLP area. A minority of SSLPs commissioned services from the mainstream providers under a service level agreement (meaning that they funded an extra post in the mainstream community team and then commissioned extra time from each team member for SSLP women). In a few SSLPs, Sure Start posts were created as part of an integrated team.

Some Sure Start maternity practitioners provided clinical care for a caseload of women in the SSLP area. For midwives, this was usually intensive one-to-one care for vulnerable women with high support needs, such as teenagers, homeless women, or women with problematic addiction, and it replaced antenatal and postnatal care (but rarely intra-partum care) from mainstream providers. For health visitors, this was usually a generic caseload of women in the SSLP replacing mainstream health visiting. A key benefit of one-to-one care was enabling a relationship of trust to develop between client and practitioner.

More commonly, Sure Start maternity professionals provided extra services for women in the SSLP, while mainstream midwives and health visitors continued to provide normal clinical care. Midwives who also carried a Sure Start caseload had less time available to provide these extra services.

What were their new ways of working?

Sure Start brought about dramatic changes in the work of maternity professionals, including:

- adopting a public health remit;
- the type of catchment for which they were responsible;
- multi-disciplinary and multi-agency work.

Public health

Whereas traditionally, maternity services operated on a clinical model of care, focussed on risk assessment and intervention, Sure Start midwives and health visitors used a public health approach that aimed to identify and meet each family's wider social and psychological needs. They made access to healthcare easier and less formal, working flexibly to offer choice in the type and delivery of services.

Catchment

Traditionally, health visiting and community midwifery services were attached to general practitioner (GP) practices and therefore clients were scattered over a wide area. For SSLP services their clients were primarily families resident in the SSLP area. Advantages were:

- maternity staff got to know the local background and became trusted by the communities;
- group sessions encouraged and enabled women to make local friendships and build networks that could be sustained beyond group sessions;
- maternity services could be delivered to families not registered with a GP (often an issue for asylum-seeking and homeless families).

A disadvantage was a perceived unfairness to families just outside SSLP boundaries not entitled to enhanced services (although in practice many SSLPs regularly allowed families from the surrounding non-Sure Start area to use their services).

Multi-disciplinary and multi-agency working

There has always been rivalry, and relatively little contact, between midwives and health visitors, with a handover at approximately 10–14 days after birth. In SSLPs midwives and health visitors were working as part of an integrated team. This collaboration resulted in significant improvements in continuity of care between the antenatal and postnatal periods, with joint visits, efficient handovers and follow-up. The integrated nature of SSLPs teams enabled midwives and health visitors to co-work with nursery nurses, family support workers, outreach workers, healthcare assistants, home visitors, bilingual link workers, community dietitians and community psychiatric nurses. A key enabler was sharing a common base at the Sure Start centre. Co-location gave maternity and other staff informal opportunities to share knowledge and refer clients to each other. Where SSLPs delivered maternity services at satellite venues SSLP staff informally attended the clinics or groups, co-facilitated groups or led particular sessions.

To provide comprehensive maternity care, most SSLPs brought in expertise from local statutory and voluntary agencies outside the Sure Start team. Experts were invited to antenatal and postnatal groups to offer information and support on topics such as healthy eating, welfare benefits, maternal mental health, the emotional aspects of having a baby and relationships. Some SSLPs funded voluntary organisations to provide a specific service for Sure Start women, such as befriending or breast-feeding counselling.

Some SSLPs used paraprofessional maternity care assistants to provide elements of services, such as breast-feeding support, freeing up midwifery or health visitor time to concentrate on specialist services. For example, one SSLP used maternity care assistants to provide practical and social support at home to women for six weeks after birth. Some professionals had difficulties adjusting to paraprofessionals, reflecting a debate going on more widely in children's services; for example, some midwives expressed concern that their role was being eroded.

Multi-agency teamwork resulted in improved referral links. The SSLP maternity staff worked with city- or county-wide services and the voluntary sector to arrange clear and efficient referrals to mainstream services for Sure Start women who needed additional support, especially on issues such as smoking cessation, domestic violence and support for women with postnatal depression.

Extra time allocated to maternity practitioners for non-clinical work enabled some to take the lead on a key maternity issue, particularly breast-feeding or postnatal depression. It allowed them to build comprehensive partnerships with all the relevant stakeholders to transform services beyond the SLLP. One SSLP created a partnership with the PCT, mental health services, social services, the acute trust, the health visiting service, and local parents to develop an integrated care pathway on postnatal depression that included training for staff, screening of women, listening visits, support groups and clearer referral paths.

What did their maternity services look like?

The themed study on maternity services (Kurtz et al., 2005: www.ness. bbk.ac.uk) explored the processes by which SSLPs followed the guidelines in implementing services. Details of the methodology are in the report.

Service format

SSLPs offered a range of antenatal and postnatal services to address key factors affecting maternal and infant health. Typical services included holistic support around preparation for parenthood, breast-feeding, smoking cessation, postnatal depression, mother–infant bonding, diet and exercise.

The key mechanisms used to deliver services were antenatal and postnatal groups, which promoted supportive relationships among the women attending. Groups often mixed maternity 'information' sessions with relaxation activities and a focus on raising self-esteem, parenting competence, and parent–infant bonding, as well as topics and activities associated with improved outcomes, such as diet during pregnancy and breast-feeding.

As well as running groups, Sure Start maternity practitioners did one-to-one work with clients, at home or by running drop-ins, and arranged efficient referrals (both within the SSLP and to mainstream services) on issues such as smoking cessation and postnatal depression. Some carried out antenatal screening for depression, and most screened postnatally for depression. In some SSLPs, mental health needs were largely met within the programme by staff trained to do 'listening visits' or (less commonly) cognitive behavioural therapy, and by running groups for women experiencing depression.

The most widespread maternity intervention was support for breast-feeding. Activities ranged from basic advice from the Sure Start midwife to establishing breast-feeding support groups and drop-ins, providing timely one-to-one support for women experiencing difficulties, running telephone helplines, and giving out incentives (such as pampering packs) or practical equipment (breast pumps and nursing bras). Many SSLPs arranged volunteer training for local women to become breast-feeding peer supporters. They attended groups and ran drop-ins, visited breast-feeding mothers at home, visited mainstream antenatal clinics or hospital wards, gave advice by telephone, and 'spread the word' at school gates. Sure Start practitioners were generally pleased with the results of peer support programmes, and valued their contribution to normalising breast-feeding in communities where there had previously been low breast-feeding rates.

Flexibility and accessibility

Mainstream services traditionally had provided antenatal clinics and classes to SSLP areas, but there were barriers to Sure Start communities attending them, including:

- services being physically inaccessible, where care was based at a distant maternity hospital and public transport was poor;
- women not liking the system of fixed appointments and long waiting times;
- women not feeling comfortable in mainstream antenatal classes where most of the people were not like them;
- some women not being confident enough to attend any group setting.

SSLPs tackled these barriers by taking services out into the community to acceptable venues and to the individual in her own home. They also offered services in more flexible ways.

Parents wanted services within pram-pushing distance. Where the SSLP had a Sure Start Centre, maternity clinics and groups were usually held there. This allowed a 'one-stop shop' approach that encouraged expectant parents to make contact with other Sure Start services. Some SSLPs tried to improve uptake by delivering maternity services in existing community venues familiar to the parents. Some SSLPs worked in partnership with a service with an established local reputation. For example, in one SSLP, the Sure Start midwife ran antenatal and postnatal groups for teenagers through an established Young Woman's Project. A potential disadvantage of using community venues was that Sure Start maternity services could become isolated, creating difficulties in offering mothers linked provision to other SSLP services. In rural communities, Sure Start antenatal sessions were often delivered by a travelling team, sometimes using a specially fitted bus as a mobile clinic.

To create more flexible services, health staff set up drop-in clinics instead of appointment-based ones, delivered both clinical care and antenatal education in women's own homes, and made their staff more available on an informal basis. Drop-in facilities were generally better used than traditional services for which an appointment was necessary, because the approach was informal. Flexibility was of particular value to women with chaotic lifestyles as they could not 'fail' by missing an appointment.

Many SSLPs invested their extra maternity staff time in delivering home-based antenatal and postnatal services, usually targeting women who had complex needs or lacked the confidence to attend groups, or who for cultural reasons found it difficult to leave the home. Home visiting had a major impact on improving access for families in rural communities. As well as being convenient for the women, home-based care was used as the foundation of building a relationship with women, and gaining insight into their social circumstances that might impact on pregnancy and their ability to follow advice on self-care (for example, their cooking facilities, or relationship with a partner).

Most midwives tried to be available to mothers on their own terms, by becoming well-known faces in the community. As well as offering drop-ins and home visits, many midwives (particularly if they were offering clinical care), and some health visitors, could be contacted via mobile phones and email. They encouraged calls to discuss worries promptly.

Sustaining use of universal services

Where women failed to attend scheduled mainstream maternity appointments, Sure Start midwives or health visitors contacted them. They gained an understanding of the reasons why the woman did not attend, and either mobilised Sure Start resources (such as transport, childcare or a companion) to help her overcome obstacles or provided her with care at home.

Targeted services

SSLPs tailored distinct services where they identified subsections of their population as less likely to use universal maternity services. Often this was in the form of separate antenatal and postnatal groups, or sometimes they developed peer support networks from within the community, particularly to support breast-feeding. Both approaches were used successfully to create services acceptable to teenagers and to women from ethnic minority communities. Sometimes they worked in partnership with existing young people's or community organisations. Engaging teenagers in services was a key task of the Sure Start midwife, often done by home visits, and teenagers were usually included in any caseload. Where there was existing mainstream activity around teenage pregnancy, the SSLPs concentrated on establishing effective referral pathways for pregnant teenagers into mainstream services (DfES and DoH, 2007).

Some SSLPs had significant populations of homeless women, asylum seekers, travellers or undocumented migrants. The Sure Start maternity staff worked in partnership with relevant support organisations. Some tried to gain the confidence of these vulnerable women by offering practical assistance, for example, support in applying for grants or re-housing and in finding cheap or donated baby clothes. Outreach was a key tool to making contact with pregnant women who might not otherwise access maternity services, for example taking services to a traveller site. Homelessness was a criterion for inclusion in a Sure Start midwife's caseload, and regular strategies to reach the homeless were knocking on the doors of hostels, or forging links with accommodation providers.

A few SSLPs with a high prevalence of substance misuse developed specialist services. Sometimes women with problematic addiction were included in the clinical caseload of a Sure Start midwife; or the midwife built up trust with the client before referring her on to the mainstream hospital-based multi-disciplinary substance misuse clinic; or Sure Start maternity staff had strong links with substance misuse workers either within the SSLP or at a local voluntary agency.

Lessons learned

- Flexible local services were more accessible to disadvantaged women than traditional services.
- Delivering services on a neighbourhood basis, and having extra time to spend with disadvantaged women, increased the ability of practitioners to build relationships with individuals and communities.
- Extra investment was a key ingredient in enabling enhanced support for vulnerable pregnant women and new mothers, whose needs were not met by overstretched traditional services.

- Team working between midwives and health visitors, especially when they worked from the same building, assisted the smooth handover of women between the antenatal and postnatal periods.
- Marginalised women's access to a range of appropriate help and support was improved by the creation of strong referral links between maternity and other services.
- Co-location of maternity practitioners with other health and social care staff improved multi-disciplinary teamwork.
- Joined-up working on maternity issues was more successful where the participation of the maternity services was built into the programme structure and systems from the outset.
- Some maternity practitioners were enthusiastic and innovative in working in new ways to meet the needs of their communities, but others (especially in the mainstream services) resented the implication that they were not already meeting women's needs and resisted change.

Conclusion

The experience of delivering maternity services in SSLPs showed that offering antenatal and postnatal care in children's centres is likely to improve access and uptake of other services. Benefits are likely to be greater where midwives and health visitors work as part of a multi-disciplinary team meeting the needs of parents and young children rather than just using the centre as a base for delivering services. Partnership working should include making full use of referral opportunities within the children's centre. Maternity services need to participate in designing protocols for sharing information and use shared records, with appropriate safeguards for confidentiality. Commissioners and managers of children's centres should ensure that midwifery and health visiting managers are included from the earliest opportunity in decisions about the design of children's centres and services.

Commissioners should, however, be realistic about the limitations on improvements in service delivery to be expected from relocating community midwifery and health visiting from GP surgeries into children's centres. Benefits reported by SSLPs derived from the significant financial investment in staff that enabled maternity practitioners to spend more time with vulnerable clients, to deliver more flexible services, and to offer additional services. In the context of mainstream staff shortages and financial constraints, none of these improvements is likely to occur simply through the transfer of existing staff from one venue to another.

References

CPHVA (Community Practitioners and Health Visitors Association)/Amicus (2006) *Who Cares? Campaign Pack*. (www.amicus-cphva.org)

CPHVA (Community Practitioners and Health Visitors Association)/Amicus (2007) 'New research reveals more than half of health visitors are making fewer home visits'. Press Release, 15 April. (Available at www.amicus-cphva.org)

Curtis, C., Ball, L. and Kirkham, M. (2003) *Why Do Midwives Leave? Talking to Managers*. London: Women's Informed Childbearing and Health Research Group.

DfEE (Department for Education and Employment) (1999) *A Guide for Second-Wave Programmes*. London: DfEE.

DfES (Department for Education and Skills) (2006) *Sure Start Children's Centres: Practice Guidance*. London: DfES. (Available at www.surestart.gov.uk/publications/? Document=1854)

DfES and DoH (Department for Education and Skills & Department of Health) (2007) *Multi-agency Working to Support Pregnant Teenagers: A Midwifery Guide to Partnership Working with Connexions and Other Agencies*. London: DfES. (Available at www.everychildmatters.gov.uk/_files/C5A2FA08979FF29B1711ED9D8F631BF6.pdf)

DoH (Department of Health) (2007) *Maternity Matters: Choice, Access and Continuity of Care in a Safe Service*. London: DoH. (Available at www.dh.gov.uk/en/Publications andstatistics/Publications/PublicationsPolicyAndGuidance/DH_073312)

DoH and DfES (Department of Health & Department for Education and Skills) (2004) *National Service Framework for Children, Young People and Maternity Services*. London: DoH. (Available at www.dh.gov.uk/en/Publicationsandstatistics/Publications/PublicationsPolicyAndGuidance/Browsable/DH_4094336)

Her Majesty's Treasury (2004) *Spending Review: Public Service Agreements 2005–2008*. London: HM Treasury.

House of Commons Health Committee (2007) 'NHS deficits: first report of session 2006–07: Vol. 2 Oral and written evidence', *House of Commons papers 73–II 2006–07*. London: The Stationery Office. (Available at www.publications.parliament.uk/pa/cm 200506/cmselect/cmhealth/1204/1204we41.htm)

Kurtz, Z., McLeish, J., Arora, A. and Ball, M. (2005) *Maternity Services Provision in Sure Start Local Programmes: Report No 12*. London: HMSO. (Available at www.ness.bbk.ac.uk/documents/activities/implementation/1188.pdf)

MCWP (Maternity Care Working Party) (2006) *Modernising Maternity Care: A Commissioning Toolkit for England*, 2nd edition. National Childbirth Trust, Royal College of Midwives, Royal College of Obstetricians and Gynaecologists. (Available at www.nct.org.uk)

Parkinson, C. (2007) 'NHS cuts "hit antenatal classes"', *BBC online*. 26th March. (Available at http://news.bbc.co.uk/1/hi/health/6468331.stm)

Suggested further reading

DfES and DoH (Department for Education and Skills & Department of Health) (2007) *Multi-agency Working to Support Pregnant Teenagers: A Midwifery Guide to Partnership Working with Connexions and Other Agencies*. London: DfES.

DoH and DfES (Department of Health & Department for Education and Skills) (2004) *National Service Framework for Children, Young People and Maternity Services*. London: DoH.

Kurtz, Z., McLeish, J., Arora, A. and Ball, M. (2005) *Maternity Services Provision in Sure Start Local Programmes: Report No 12*. London: HMSO.

7 Early Learning, Play and Childcare in Sure Start Local Programmes

Angela Anning

This chapter:

- examines the remit for Sure Start Early Learning (EL), Play (P) and Childcare (CC) services
- discusses policy and research contexts for these services
- describes examples of good practice
- identifies lessons learned.

Key questions:

- How can a balance be maintained between the needs of children and their parents in EL, P and CC services?
- How can practitioners maintain quality whilst promoting innovation in the services?
- What are the key indicators of service proficiency and effectiveness?

Like maternity services, early learning, play and childcare services were pivotal to the success of SSLPs because they provided a gateway to the take-up of other services. Centre-based costs were high for early learning, play and childcare services, with the need for specialist premises and high staffing ratios. They accounted for 12 per cent of expenditure in the first year of SSLPs, rising to 20 per cent in the third and fourth years.

What programmes were expected to do

The remit for early learning and play services included improving young children's ability to learn, by encouraging stimulating and enjoyable play, improving language skills, and through early identification supporting children with learning difficulties. Services were to be reconfigured to offer open-access drop-in centres providing high-quality play resources and part-time places in early years settings (private, statutory or voluntary) for all 3-year-olds. Targets were:

- at least 90 per cent of children to achieve normal speech and language development at 18 months and 3 years;
- 100 per cent of children in Sure Start areas to have access to good-quality play and early learning opportunities, giving them a flying start to school.

Childcare was to focus on facilitating the take-up of jobs, education and training for parents, and on offering crèche facilities to parents attending family support or literacy schemes. Criteria for maintaining, improving or setting up new childcare included: conformity with the requirements of the Children Act of 2004 and New Standards for provision; offering high-quality learning experiences appropriate for the age of the children; building on children's natural curiosity; and promoting social, emotional and cognitive development.

The policy context

The national policy context for early education (including play) and childcare is outlined in Chapter 1. But historically in the UK responsibility for early childhood services was split between: local authority Social Services departments for childcare, including childminding, and for under-fives 'at risk'; local education authorities for 3–7-year-olds in nursery and primary schools; voluntary sector organisations for playgroups and family support programmes; and health authorities for healthcare for all young children and their families. Provision was patchy depending on the history of local authority priorities. Services were fragmented, with young children spending periods of time outside their homes before they started school with childminders or relatives, in playgroups, family centres or nursery and reception classes in primary schools.

Families encountered professionals in each setting with different qualifications and beliefs. Staff worked to a range of training, pay and conditions, career structures, holiday entitlements and supervisory models. Consequently, a nursery officer in a family centre and a teacher in a reception class brought different knowledge and expertise to joint working in SSLP multi-agency teams. Moreover, a DfES survey in 2003 reported on the low levels of qualifications in early childhood services: 64 per cent of staff were not qualified beyond Level 2 National Vocational Qualifications and 13 per cent were unqualified (DfES, 2003: 17–18), with under-representation of men and black and minority ethnic groups. This was the uncomfortable reality for SSLP teams charged with improving inherited services and planning to deliver new services.

What did we already know about what works?

As described in Chapter 1, the Sure Start vision was underpinned by evidence of 'what works'[1] in early intervention programmes.

In early learning the influential Effective Provision of Pre-School Education (EPPE) Project reported that all children who attended some kind of pre-school (even if it was part time) – but particularly those from a disadvantaged context – demonstrated better cognitive and social competence outcomes when they started school (Sylva et al., 2003).

High-quality pre-school provision was characterised by an approach to pedagogy which promoted:

- episodes of adult/child 'shared sustained thinking', open-ended questioning and formative feedback to children involved in learning episodes;
- employment of practitioners with a clear grasp of child development and knowledge of the curriculum;
- practitioners with shared aims for children's learning with their parents;
- transparent behaviour policies and practices;
- play activities where adults engaged as play partners and where practitioners tuned into and accommodated the knowledge and culture of parents (Siraj-Blatchford et al., 2004).

The group settings most likely to provide high-quality pre-school provision, and to promote better outcomes for children, were integrated care and education settings and nursery schools. But the small sample of integrated settings in the study included well-resourced centres of excellence set up by the government in the late 1990s to model good practice, so we must be cautious about generalising EPPE findings to all integrated settings. Nevertheless, the findings encouraged the government to pursue a policy of integrating care and education.

However, equally important for promoting good outcomes for the children was the learning environment of the home. Where parents engaged in learning activities with their children, regardless of parents' social class or level of education, children's social and cognitive attainments were enhanced.

In a parallel project, Sammons et al. (2003) investigated good practice in provision for children with diverse needs. Good practice included stringent systems in place to identify, respond to and provide appropriate support/treatment for children with special educational needs or disabilities, in particular at points of transition and transfer to school.

The challenges of working with children and families with special educational needs or disabilities in SSLP areas were explored in the NESS themed study, A Better Start (Pinney, 2006). Pinney identified as important:

- the critical role of family support in overcoming barriers to access to specialist services and to support families at times of crisis;
- targeting and offering specialist services (such as speech and language therapy and occupational therapy) on a preventative basis;
- routine procedures and protocols for including children with diverse needs in all mainstream early learning, play and childcare services.

Research on the impact of childcare on young children is more contentious. Melhuish (2004) cited evidence that where children attend high-quality childcare, they demonstrate enhanced social and cognitive effects. He summarised the characteristics of good quality childcare as:

- well-trained staff committed to their work with children;
- facilities that are safe and sanitary and accessible to parents;
- ratios and group sizes that allow staff to interact appropriately with children;
- supervision that maintains consistency;
- staff development that ensures continuity, stability and improving quality;
- provision of appropriate learning opportunities for children.

But Belsky (1999) argued that where children in the US experienced poor-quality day care, characterised by emotionally detached caring, of more than 12 hours a week (particularly where they were living in poverty or in disadvantaged home settings) they were likely to display aggressive behaviours and less social competence when they started school. More recently in the UK, a study of the neighbourhood nursery initiative (La Valle et al., 2007) reported that children who had attended day care (mostly in Sure Start areas) showed more aggression, but also more social competence, at school entry. One of the greatest challenges in childcare is settling children into group settings. Elfer et al. (2003) argued that young children have the right to bond with a key worker within the resources and structures of a well-managed system of daycare.

A full discussion of evidence on effectiveness of early childhood services and underpinning theoretical models is in the NESS Themed Study, *The Quality of Early Learning, Play and Childcare Services in SSLPs* (Anning et al., 2005) (available at www.surestart.gov.uk or www.ness.bbk.uk)

What did Sure Start local programme early learning and play and childcare services look like?

The challenge was to retain proven effective elements of inherited services while developing innovative services responsive to local communities' needs and preferences. Services had to be flexible, accessible and affordable. And teams had to maintain quality while experimenting with new ways of working. So what did services look like?

Early learning

In Sure Start early learning experiences, children received support for speech and language and emotional development and extra opportunities for physical and literacy development. But there was less emphasis on children's cognitive development, and some learning activities were ill matched to very young children's capabilities.

In the example of a successful early learning activity below, the purpose of sessions was explained clearly to parents. The quality of relationships between parents, staff and children was a priority. The sessions were held regularly and staff prepared the environment and resources carefully. Young children were encouraged to learn from interacting with each other, with adults paying close attention and reflecting on evidence of children learning together. Parents were encouraged to share what they had learned with friends and extended family, taking home video-tapes of their children's learning.

The Growing Together Group

Aims   The group offered a weekly opportunity for babies and toddlers who were mobile to engage in heuristic play with everyday materials. The aims were to offer high-quality play experiences, involve parents in observing and supporting their child's early learning and to enrich child–parent relationships. The SSLP combined a voluntary-sector family centre (following a social services 'rescue' approach to service delivery) and a medical pre-school unit (offering universal services). Practitioners' experiences were in psychoanalysis, family support, early education and adult education. The multi-agency team was committed to developing a shared approach, but the process of integration had generated debate and stress.

What happened   Staff set up sparkling fabrics, comfortable cushions and tactile everyday materials, displayed attractively on the floor. Materials offered open-ended play opportunities. Everyday objects and natural materials modelled alternatives to commercial toys.

After greeting parents and children, the staff ensured that everyone was comfortably seated in a circle of floor cushions and chairs around the heuristic play equipment. Parents were quietly reminded of the purpose and format of the session. The adult role was as supportive and engaged observer, rather than active involvement in the children's play.

Soon, everyone fell silent as the toddlers began to explore the materials. The children were absorbed in play, mostly managing interactions with their peers without adult interference.

Observations   Jake's mother told us that she was initially concerned about his aggression towards other children. Regular attendance at the sessions had allowed Jake to socialise and interact with his peers, and reduce his aggressive behaviour.

Jake, aged 16 months, left his mother's side and toddled towards a basket of hair-rollers. He picked them up one at a time and brushed them against his cheek, then against the palm of his hand. He turned around and grabbed a cardboard tube, through which he began posting the rollers, frowning with concentration. Each time a roller emerged from the tube, Jake giggled and looked towards his mother. She responded with nods and smiles of encouragement. Several times Jake demonstrated positive social behaviours, such as handing another child an object.

Reflections   After 45 minutes the practitioner drew the session to an end. The group tidied away and gathered for a drink and a snack. Créche workers supervised the children. Staff and parents discussed their observations of children, reflecting on their implication for the child's development, and considering ways of supporting the child's learning at home. One mum commented:

> 'Coming here, it's helped me to understand why she does things and how I can support her learning better. Things like when we're at the café she always gets the sugar cubes out the bowl and stacks them up. I don't get mad now; I know a bit more about why she's wanting to do it.'

The sessions were documented by parents or staff using a video camera, and recordings were replayed to reflect on significant episodes. This documentation was a powerful tool for sharing professional knowledge about early learning and play and enabled parents to take the video recording home to share their child's experiences with family and friends.

Impact   One practitioner commented:

> 'We're really getting to those relationships. By observing the babies, adults are tuning in, and we see a lot of parents really seeing their children as individuals ... Parents notice things that their babies are doing and suddenly this baby is very much an individual. And that helps that parent to really connect with their child. I think that is such a good thing. To support that attachment.'

A mum said:

> 'It's a totally relaxing time for us both ... I think it's the one time she can have me, without my other daughter, just for herself. And with the baby coming it's probably OK for us just to be peaceful here together for these sessions.'

(Anning et al., 2005: 92–6)

Play

In Sure Start play experiences, children benefited from many new experiences, including outings, toy libraries, outdoor and physical exercise often shared with parents; but there was tension in some services between different professional and community beliefs about the role of play in promoting early learning.

The example below is of a play party to encourage literacy and library use. It was delivered from a community library in an ethnically diverse area. It demonstrates the benefits of:

- building positively on diversity in communities;
- recruiting staff representative of that diversity;
- a whole-team approach towards a shared vision;
- fun learning together as practitioners, parents and children;
- parents and children sharing early literacy experiences.

A play party with early literacy experience

Aims   The SSLP worked hard to develop positive relationships with community and religious groups. A local recruitment policy ensured that throughout the staffing structure the team were representative of these groups.

A comprehensive training programme was in place for volunteers and workers to learn about the importance of play for young children. Every fortnight, the programme held a play party at the local library with the aim of encouraging local families to use the library services. Every three months a large-scale play event was organised to attract new families to SSLP services.

What happened   For one event children and parents were invited to bring their bear to an afternoon of fun and food at a teddy bears' picnic. Over one hundred children and their families, representing the rich diversity of local cultures, attended. The whole Sure Start team were present to net-work with the families and, where relevant, broker access to universal or specialist services.

The focus was on fun. Families received a warm welcome from staff and were invited to decorate a party mask. At one point a mass of bubbles filled the room and the children screamed with excitement as they tried to catch them. The atmosphere was relaxed and informal as families enjoyed the party together. Everyone gathered together for story time. Practitioners shared lively stories and songs about bears, using props and visual effects. A life-sized 'bear' appeared, which the more confident children were encouraged to greet. Other children watched from the safety of their mothers' arms. Families sat down at tables where staff served them with food and drinks. The shared feast was the highlight of the afternoon and was celebrated as such by the staff.

The impact   A grandmother present with her daughter and grand-children said:

'I think the staff here are wonderful, I really do. And they represent all the cultures we have in this area – it's very multicultural here and Sure Start has really helped those cultures to come together for days like this. It's brilliant.'

The SSLP team recognised the importance of parents and children sharing early literacy experiences. One mum said:

'I think the library days are good for getting my child interested in books and nursery rhymes. They are often the same books and rhymes she has at the nursery. I get to know them and we can sing the songs at home. The baby is starting to know them too.'

(Anning et al., 2005: 102–105)

Childcare

For parents, Sure Start childcare allowed them to work or be trained as well as offering a break; but parents often wanted sessional rather than full day care provision. Many SSLPs relied on buying in childcare from other providers, particularly when a neighbourhood nursery initiative (aimed at expanding day care in partnership with private providers in the most disadvantaged areas of England) was introduced in 2000.

In the example below, a newly built day care centre in a rural setting was designed around extensive consultation with local communities to provide flexible and affordable childcare for working parents. It illustrates the importance of promoting positive relationships between parents and providers and of passing daily information about young children between home and the group settings. The staff responded to individual children's preferences for physical care, nurturing and play activities, and recognised the importance for children in group settings of making friends.

Promoting positive parenting at a day care centre

Aims   The nursery was in a small market town serving as a hub for isolated villages and farms. One mum commented:

'The nursery opening has been great – a real godsend. And it came at the perfect time for me. If it hadn't opened I wouldn't have been able to go back to work. There's no other nurseries for babies round here.'

Although a key aim for the nursery was to provide childcare to benefit parents, the staff emphasised the children's well-being as critical. Practitioners visited children at home before they started nursery, and a careful admissions procedure was planned with parents to minimise stress for the children as they settled into the centre.

Staff ensured that parents felt welcome and always made time to talk with them. One mum said:

'The staff are great – like gold-dust, really. You know that you can always come in and talk to them if you have a question or are worried about anything, or just to have a chat. The atmosphere in here is lovely.'

Close attention was paid to children's routines and the needs of individual families. One mum commented:

'When Daniel first started here he was only three months. I was a bit worried about his routine; you know that he'd have one at home and one for nursery and what would happen. But the staff were great. They just said "Tell us what you do at home and we'll follow the same routine here." And they do. It's working really well and Daniel loves it here.'

For parents the social aspect of the nursery was important. A mother said:

'Jack's always been very confident and he just loves it here. To me that's the most important part of it – that he's learning to mix and the social side of it. And we like the fact that the children are mixing with other ages. It feels more homely.'

What happened The purpose-built nursery was attractive and well resourced with good-quality foundation stage equipment. Practitioners planned for and supported a range of play experiences, both inside and outside. They observed the children's interests and development and kept detailed individual records, always available for parents to look at and contribute to.

The practitioners were responsive to the changing dynamics of the children in the nursery. More babies were attending the nursery. By analysing observations, practitioners identified that the needs of babies, toddlers and pre-school children could not always be met in the same area. They created an area for babies to crawl and explore in safety, divided from the rest of the room by low screens.

We asked practitioners to encourage the children to record their favourite things in the nursery using an instant camera. We also sent a bear to the children for them to show him around their nursery. The children's photographs and comments identified their favourite toys and experiences. Practitioners were not surprised by the children's choice of favourite things, an indication that they knew the children well.

The children included photos of their friends amongst their favourite things. One child immediately introduced the bear to his friends. Another child showed the bear where the babies slept.

The 3-year-olds' responses suggested that routines were important. They took photographs of the bathrooms, the kitchen, the sleeping area and the snack table. One child was keen to show the bear where he could have a rest and curled up with him on the cushions. Outside play was also important to them.

Observation   A new baby had recently been born in Emily's family. Emily frequently talked about the baby at nursery and the practitioners recognised the significance of this life change for her. When it was Emily's turn to show the bear around, she immediately took him to the block area. She built an enclosure into which she carefully placed the bear, telling the practitioner that she had made a cot. Emily then took the bear to the snack table where she pretended to give him some milk.

(Anning et al., 2005: 109–113)

Key messages

The characteristics of good-quality early learning, play and childcare SSLP services were:

- responsiveness to local communities' needs and preferences;
- ethos which positively valued the home culture and competencies of the children and parents who use them;
- commitment to recognising and promoting the quality of relationships between children, practitioners, parents and carers;
- commitment to developing inter-agency links and multi-agency teamwork;
- clear strategies for the recruitment, training and retention of appropriate staffing;
- commitment to the early identification and safeguarding of vulnerable families and children;
- provision for the emotional and physical well-being of all adults and children;
- clear understanding of and high-quality provision for promoting child development and learning;
- systematic evaluation of the impact and cost benefits of services;

- rigorous systems for recording, monitoring and analysing the use of services by individuals and families;
- maintenance of a balance between concern for empowering parents, staff and children.

The challenges to maintaining services of this quality were:

- management of multi-agency teamwork;
- design of appropriate activities to promote learning in children under 3;
- recruitment, retention and retraining of staff;
- training for managers to enable them to lead and manage innovative, proficient and effective services.

Conclusion

Early evidence from the evaluation of the Sure Start intervention indicated that after several years of enhanced services, 3-year-olds in the SSLP areas were not achieving the targets of 'normal' speech and language development (NESS, 2005). In fact, in lone, single-parent families, 3-year-olds were scoring lower on verbal ability than children in comparative groups outside SSLP areas. However, measures of parenting did show small but significant gains, with less maternal negative behaviours towards 3-year-olds and more acceptance of their behaviours. In the long run we would expect better parenting to result in improved child outcomes; and more recent evidence of impact on the parents in Sure Start areas shows a variety of beneficial effects for children and their families, when children were 3 years old (NESS, 2008).

SSLPs worked hard to reach the target of 100 per cent of under-fours in their areas having access to play and learning opportunities. But in their haste to expand services, and knit together provision from the private, voluntary and maintained sector, it was difficult to maintain high quality. A further problem was that reach-figures for services were disappointing, particularly for the most vulnerable and at-risk families for whom the Sure Start vision was created. Universal provision was not matched with universal uptake of costly services. This may be one reason why child outcomes were not significantly better than expected.

Childcare was also expanded, but many parents were ambivalent about returning to work or training while their children were so young. They used sessional respite places. But many full-time day care places were not taken up. SSLPs struggled to maintain good quality crèche provision, partly because of the volume of under 3-year-olds to be accommodated in short-term placements whilst parents attended 2-hour group sessions or requested respite care. Because many SSLPs franchised the staffing of crèches to outside agencies, managers struggled to ensure the consistency or quality of crèche staffing.

However, as this chapter demonstrates, many innovative services were created. The hope is that lessons learned from the experiences of SSLPs will provide guidance to those designing and delivering EL, P and CC services from children's centres.

Note

1 The phrase 'what works' was common in policy documents during this period. Implicit in the way is it used in this chapter is the notion of relativism. SSLPs and services were successful in different ways, in different contexts, for different groups of people at different points in their communities' and services' histories.

References

Anning, A., Chesworth, E. and Spurling, L. (2005) *The Quality of Early Learning, Play and Childcare Services in Sure Start Local Programmes.* NESS Research Report 09. Nottingham: DfES (Available at www.ness.bbk.ac.uk)

Belsky, J. (1999) 'Interactional and contextual determinants of attachment security', in J. Cassidy and P.R. Shayer (eds) *Handbook of Attachment: Theory, Research and Clinical Applications.* New York: Guildford.

DfES (Department for Education and Science) (2003) *Recruitment and Retention of Childcare, Early Years and Playworkers: Research Study,* Rolfe, M., Metcalfe, H., Anderson, T. and Meadows, P. (Research Report 409). Nottingham: DfES.

Elfer, P., Goldschmeid, E. and Selleck, D. (2003) *Key Person Relationships in the Nursery.* London: Sage.

La Valle, I., Smith, R., Purdon, S., Bell, A., Dearden, L., Shaw, J. and Sibieta, L. (2007) *National Evaluation of the Neighbourhood Nursery Initiative: Impact Report,* Publication Code SSU/2007/FR/020. London: HMSO. (Available at www.surestart.gov.uk)

Melhuish, E. (2004) *A Literature Review of the Impact of Early Provision upon Young Children, with Emphasis Given to Children from Disadvantaged Backgrounds: Report to the Controller and Auditor General.* London: National Audit Office.

NESS (National Evaluation of Sure Start) (2005) *Early Impacts of the Sure Start Local Programmes on Children and Families, Report 013.* Nottingham: DfES. (Available at www.ness.bbk.ac.uk)

NESS (National Evaluation of Sure Start) (2008) *The Impact of Sure Start Local Programmes on Three Year Olds and their Families.* Nottingham: DfES (Available at www.ness.bbk.ac.uk)

Pinney, A. (2006) *A Better Start: Sure Start Local Programmes' Work with Children and Families with Special Needs and Disabilities.* NESS/2005/FR/009. Nottingham: DfES (Available at www.ness.bbk.ac.uk)

Sammons, P., Taggart, B., Smees, R., Sylva, K., Melhuish, E., Siraj-Blatchford, I. and Elliott, K. (2003) *The Early Years Transition and Special Educational Needs Project.* London: Special Educational Needs Division of the DfES.

Siraj-Blatchford, I., Sylva, K., Muttock, S., Gillian, R. and Bell, D. (2002) *Researching Effective Pedagogy in the Early Years.* Research Report No 356, Department for Education and Skills. London: HMSO. Also available from London Institute of Education, Bedford Way, London.

Sylva, K., Sammons, P., Melhuish, E., Siraj-Blatchford, I., Taggart, B. and Elliott, K. (2003) *The Effective Provision of Pre-School Education (EPPE) Project: Findings from the Pre-School Period.* Research Brief No. RBX 15-03. London: Department for Education and Skills. Also available from London Institute of Education, Bedford Way, London.

Suggested further reading

Anning, A., Chesworth, E. and Spurling, L. (2005) *The Quality of Early Learning, Play and Childcare Services in Sure Start Local Programmes.* NESS Research Report 009. Nottingham: DfES.

Melhuish, E. (2004) *A Literature Review of the Impact of Early Provision upon Young Children, with Emphasis Given to Children from Disadvantaged Backgrounds: Report to the Controller and Auditor General.* London: National Audit Office.

Sylva, K., Sammons, P., Melhuish, E., Siraj-Blatchford, I., Taggart, B. and Elliott, K. (2003) *The Effective Provision of Pre-School Education (EPPE) Project: Findings from the Pre-School Period.* Research Brief No. RBX 15-03. London: Department for Education and Skills. Also available from London Institute of Education, Bedford Way, London.

8 Speech and Language Therapy

Veronica Sawyer, Caroline Pickstone and David Hall

This chapter:

- reviews current knowledge about language acquisition and early literacy
- examines the ways in which professionals, in particular speech and language therapists (SaLTs), have responded
- explores how Sure Start Local Programmes (SSLPs) approached developing children's communications skills
- discusses implications for policy and practice.

Key questions:

o What benefits does a multi-agency team approach bring to promoting language acquisition?

o How can we ensure all children start school with a positive approach to literacy?

o How are generic and specialist skills within a multi-agency team best deployed to maximise impact of services on their users?

What do we know about speech and language development?

Oral language difficulties predispose a child to difficulties with written language and to educational failure (Tallal and Benasich, 2002). Children growing up in disadvantaged circumstances are especially vulnerable (McLoyd, 1998). McLoyd demonstrated a widening gap, with increasing age from 10 to 36 months in the vocabulary growth of a sample of children from three social backgrounds. From 18 months the differences begin to diverge, so that by 36 months 13 children from 'professional' family backgrounds had accumulated over 1000 words; 23 children from 'working class' backgrounds over 700 words; and 6 children from 'welfare' backgrounds over 500 words (see Hart and Risley, 1995: 234). McLoyd related these differences to the amount of exposure to language in children from the three different backgrounds, measured by differences in the estimated cumulative millions of words addressed to the children within each sample (see Hart and Risley, 1995: 252). There are significant genetic influences on language development (Dale et al. 1998) but it is also critically dependent on interactions with parents and other carers (Rutter, 1999). Thus a social gradient in language achievement is evident even by the age of two (see Feinstein, 2003); and as argued above the differences in attainment have been linked to the poorer quality and quantity of language exposure in comparison with more fortunate children (Hart and Risley, 1995; 1999).

Strategies used by adults to support language acquisition in infancy and early childhood are delineated in Table 8.1. Greater use of such strategies with disadvantaged children would be expected to accelerate their language development and raise their educational achievement, though the size of such benefits is still uncertain.

There is no absolute distinction between 'normal', 'delayed' and 'disordered' speech and language development (Bishop, 1997). Screening speech and language 'delay' followed by one-to-one speech and language therapy do not make best use of scarce therapy skills (Law et al., 1998). The emphasis has switched to the context for learning (Bronfenbrenner, 1979) and enhancing the quality of children's language exposure by promoting responsive parent–child

Table 8.1   Adult strategies to support language acquisition (drawing on Fey, 1986; Girolametto et al., 2003; and Mahoney and MacDonald, 2004)

	Examples of approaches	Suggested benefits
Child-oriented strategies	Follow the child's lead by talking about the same topic and attending to the same activity. Waiting for the child to respond. Pace of language-use to allow time to process language. Scaffolding to child's level of play performance.	Shared focus of attention. Adult is often positioned at same eye level as the child. Supporting child to achieve skills.
Responses that promote interaction	Encourage the child to interact by engaging child in conversation. Including open questions, encouraging turn-taking. Use of comment rather than mainly questions.	Maintaining attention. Encouraging child to use language to initiate and reply. Skills in conversational turn-taking. Opportunities for initiation.
Modelling of language	Providing good models of language, including labelling, and models of uses of vocabulary and concepts and grammatical forms. Scaffolding to child's level of language performance.	Opportunities for child to build on language skills through imitation.

interaction, development of language strategies (see Table 8.1), and enhancement of day care and early years staff skills (Girolametto et al., 2003).

Children in families whose first language is not English have varying needs. Some are exposed to their heritage language plus English. A bilingual environment of itself does not disadvantage, and indeed may facilitate, language development. However, some children reach school age with little or no knowledge of English and may benefit from earlier support (Bialystok, 2001).

The likelihood of children being 'non-readers' or 'poor readers' at age 7 is strongly related to social class. Early literacy is related to parental involvement (Nutbrown et al., 2005), exposure to books, listening to

Table 8.2   The ORIM framework (Nutbrown et al., 2005: 37)

1. Provides *Opportunities* to read texts and attempt writing; for example, by drawing attention to environmental print.
2. Gives *Recognition* to children's early literacy achievements.
3. Promotes *Interaction* with more proficient literacy users, usually through facilitation rather than by instruction;
4. Provides *Models* of what it is to use literacy.

stories, sharing picture books, drawing, colouring and early writing and awareness of environmental print. Projects like Bookstart aim to promote a love of books by providing opportunities for very young children to enjoy books (Moore and Wade, 2003).

Prerequisites for literacy include the capacity to distinguish qualities of the sounds of language (Goswami and Bryant, 1990) – *phonological awareness*. This is important *before* children begin to read. *Phonemic awareness* is an aspect of phonological awareness, involving conscious awareness of the elemental speech sounds of a spoken language; it develops further with teaching that links sounds and written words (DfES, 2007). Table 8.2 outlines the ORIM (Opportunities–Recognition–Interaction–Models) approach, drawing on the work of Nutbrown et al. (2005), to promoting early literacy (Hannon, 1995).

What did speech and language services in Sure Start local programmes look like?

Improvement in speech and language acquisition and pre-literacy skills was a goal of SSLPs from their inception. Law and Harris (2001) emphasised that speech and language development initiatives should not be separated from the overall framework of a Sure Start programme. It was important to take a holistic approach including parent skills, the home environment, the parental network of social contacts, community resources and the child's health.

The material in this chapter is based on a qualitative study undertaken in 15 contrasting SSLPs, during 2005-06, when Sure Start programmes were well established. We focus first on the changing roles of Sure Start staff and then give examples of service activities. Unless otherwise stated, quotes are taken from the report on the study (Sawyer et al., 2007).

Roles of Sure Start professionals

Speech and language therapists (SaLTs)

Recent research has prompted SaLTs to embrace a more public health oriented approach emphasising prevention, promotion of optimum development and early identification and referral of problems (Royal College of Speech and Language Therapists, 2006). The approach aims to:

- exclude other problems such as hearing loss, autism spectrum disorder or general learning disability;
- identify any fundamental abnormality of language processing (often called specific language impairment);
- assess the child's difficulties and offer appropriate advice, therapy or treatment.

In SSLPs, SaLTs shifted from the traditional clinical practice role of one-to-one assessment and therapy to grasp opportunities for prevention. They adopted two main strategies.

First, they collaborated with other disciplines, including nursery officers, midwives, health visitors, early years librarians, teaching assistants and teachers. They shared their understanding of how children learn to listen and communicate, how to recognise emerging language development problems that might have long-term educational significance, and how to facilitate young children's interest in speech and language. Activities involved individual contact with parents and children, and group sessions.

Second, they provided support for and consultation, with SSLP staff who worked daily with children without the need for formal referrals. A teacher said: '... if I've done all [I can] to develop a child's speech and vocabulary without success, I need someone to refer to. In the Children's Centre I have that availability of expertise within the centre, who may not be there all the time, but is a known specific person ... [the Centre] is a hub ... with resources and expertise'.

Parents appreciated this approach because it often saved them a long wait for an appointment at a clinic. Staff valued the gaining of specialist knowledge, which enhanced their expertise and self-esteem, and SaLTs felt they were using their time effectively.

Screening for identifying and managing language delay was limited. For example, we found no arrangements for hearing tests at any of the 15 SSLPs. They referred families to a hospital audiology department. One member of SSLP staff said: 'There is no need to worry [about hearing problems] as they all have newborn testing now'. She was clearly not aware that newborn screening detects only half of all childhood cases (Fortnum et al., 2001).

Many parents perceived referral to a SaLT as criticism of their parenting abilities and even an accusation of neglect (Glogowska and Campbell, 2004). Some parents found it hard to understand the extent to which their child was delayed compared with population norms, particularly in poor neighbourhoods where many children have language delay. One parent understood her child's language delay only when a SaLT demonstrated the child's difficulties.

Midwives and health visitors

Modern midwives are interested in psychosocial issues and child development, such as early 'bonding', attachment and early language acquisition (see Chapter 7). One midwife stressed an increasing interest in: '... developmental things, talking [to mums] about when the baby can see and hear, how important it is to talk to your baby even when they cannot answer you'.

Health visitors offer a service to all families, with additional support for those who need it. Health visitors attached to SSLPs did not have a fixed caseload but worked with individual families. They contributed to group sessions where parents learned about child speech and language development by observing their own and other children, exchanging experiences with other parents and learning that play is 'developing the baby's brain'. In the early days of Sure Start, such services were often not taken up until the child was around 18 months old, when parents became more aware of language development. Attitudes began to change after health visitors delivering ante- and post-natal sessions emphasised that language development begins at birth.

Staff promoting children's language development and pre-literacy skills

SaLTs and Sure Start programme managers helped parents to understand the skills and communicative abilities of babies. One SaLT produced a booklet called 'From Birth to One Year – Speech and Language Development', which emphasised that 'communication is linked to the development of other skills like hand–eye coordination, sitting, walking, eating, drinking and the senses'. It listed things the baby '*may* (rather than *should*) be doing', as age-related milestones vary widely and can worry parents (Meisels and Atkins-Burnett, 2000). Other innovations included the creation of DVDs about baby play and interaction and introducing parents to Brazelton's (Brazelton and Newton, 1995) work on new babies' communication skills.

Bookstart was one of several schemes to introduce books to babies and toddlers. A librarian said: 'They learn so quickly which way up a book goes and that it goes from front to back and not to put them in their mouths. It is quite evident when you see two children of the same age and one who hasn't had the use of books and one who has'. Health visitors took Book Start packs to families, but often lacked time to explain how to use them.

But parents were excited by the creative use of books: 'It's really good coming along here (to the library); Ellie sits still and joins in the songs, it's going to help her when she goes to school.' (Mother of 20-month-old girl) Early years librarians[1] ran play-and-learn groups and story sessions in libraries, Sure Start centres, nurseries and play groups. They aimed to present libraries as non-threatening places for parents who had problems with literacy or who felt uncomfortable in schools or other educational environments. All groups included play activities: '... complementing literacy skills with art, craft and play ... getting children working with their hands and linking it to stories, rhymes and songs so that they can make that connection'. (Librarian)

Whole team identifying and managing language delay

Staff who are not knowledgeable about language development (including some teachers) often equate speech and language problems with unclear articulation. In reality, difficulties with vocabulary, syntax, semantics and comprehension are much more likely to represent a serious long-term difficulty. Such children need to be identified and offered a comprehensive assessment to establish a diagnosis and determine their educational and therapy needs. Often parents are the first to suspect a problem, but this is not always the case, particularly for first-time parents. In SSLP day care settings, staff could observe and compare children and this enabled them to identify children whose development was not proceeding normally.

Training SSLP staff to make regular and accurate observations and diagnoses of child development (Ireton, 1990) had benefits. In addition, the SaLT identified individuals (for example, a nursery officer or nurse) to train as 'communication advisers'. They visited families, used toys (for example, 'treasure boxes'), modelled language, and generally raised parents' awareness of language development. Sometimes they worked with teachers and groups of children, visiting and observing regularly to monitor progress and offer advice.

Three levels of expertise within a staff team were defined as:

- general knowledge about communication for all staff;
- practical and applied knowledge for 'frontline' staff working directly with children;
- additional expertise for staff to advise and raise the standard of communication related services in SSLPs.

SaLT and early learning staff collaborated to set up 'stay and play' sessions during which practitioners identified children having difficulties with attention and listening. SaLTs ran special diagnostic and supportive language groups, to which children were referred, and parent consultation sessions to explain about language acquisition and activities to work on at home.

The issues raised by bilingualism and the needs of families whose first language was not English were recognised by all SSLPs, but the majority of the 15 programme managers acknowledged that more needed to be done. Many SSLPs found contacting and engaging such families difficult. There was a shortage of interpreters who had expertise in language acquisition: 'We're ... having to work via interpreters and ... maybe it's not as effective ... we need a parent group with those people who don't speak English or Bangla, have the interpreters there and go through stuff so that they can work with their children ...' (SaLT).

Many SSLPs relied on generalist staff with additional training from SaLTs: 'We've got seven bi-lingual trained childcare workers and that's just such a wonderful resource that we draw on all the time.' (SSLP manager)

Examples of group sessions designed to promote language development

In many groups, communication and pre-literacy skills were stressed and, in some, speech and language development were the central objectives.

Parent support groups focused on speech and language development

Examples of approaches to promoting speech and language using published programmes are given below.

Programmes based on schemes

- Use of the Webster Stratton approach to behaviour and parenting strategies (Webster Stratton and Mostyn, 1992): using indirect modelling and linking communication skills to behaviour management.
- Songs from the Jolly Phonics scheme.
- Modelling of book use and activities to develop children's knowledge about print; for example, developmentally graded listening bags or story bags prepared in collaboration with the SaLT.
- Combining gross motor and fine motor activities with speech and language objectives, in sessions developed by a sport and play development worker and a SaLT.
- A four-session course called *Bright Start* run by a programme manager and an educational psychologist for parents *and* practitioners, emphasising speaking, listening and language development, and the links to behaviour and cognitive development. It teaches strategies such as the use of open questions and feedback to encourage children's thinking, such as 'What do you think would happen if …?' and 'Tell me how you did that'.

Some were modelled on established programmes, such as those shown in the box below.

Examples of published programmes

High/Scope   Developed in the US by David Weikart and evaluated in the Perry Pre-school Project (Schweinhart et al., 1993) and based on Piagetian theory in regarding children as active learners.

The Reggio Emilia Approach   Evolved in the pre-schools of Reggio Emilia in Italy, influenced by Vygotsky's thesis that children and adults co-construct their theories and knowledge through their communicative relationships and interaction with their environment. The expressive arts are central vehicles for learning.

Jolly Phonics   A British commercial scheme for teaching phonics. Letter shapes and sounds are linked to pictures and words (for example, drum). A song reinforces learning the letter sound.

Peers Early Education Partnership (PEEP)   A pre-school intervention in Oxfordshire which aims to increase the educational achievement (especially literacy skills) of disadvantaged children from birth to 5 years. It forms partnerships with parents and carers by recognising and supporting their contribution to children's learning during the formative pre-school years. (www.peep.org.uk and www.dfes.gov.uk/research/data/uploadfiles/ RR489.pdf)

The Hanen Centre: early language intervention programmes   The Hanen Centre develops family-focused early language intervention programmes and learning resources for parents and professionals to develop language, social and literacy skills. Linked to the University of Toronto. (www. hanen.org)

Bookstart   A British national programme that encourages parents and carers to enjoy books with children from an early age. Three free book packs are given to children: *Bookstart* for babies age 0–12 months, *Bookstart Plus* for toddlers 18–30 months, and *My Bookstart Treasure Chest* for children 36–48 months. Health professionals have been the principle 'gifting partners'. Bookstart provides books and materials for other languages, including dual language books. (www.bookstart.co.uk)

Early Start   Basic skills for parents of children aged 0–3 years, linked to the Basic Skills Agency.
(www.literacytrust.org.uk/socialinclusion/earlyyears/earlystartpractice.html)

Some groups were delivered informally, reflecting variation in providers' views about the importance of structure and the need to cater for parents who found it hard to commit to regular attendance. 'Drop-in' sessions provided peer and professional support and advice and modelled good practice by, for example, using songs and rhymes with actions with children sitting on their parents' knees.

Parents observed how children anticipated a familiar part of a song. Puppets were used to explain the action of the mouth and tongue when words were formed. A SaLT demonstrated good eye contact and clear simple sentences with a child. One group included a song time with percussion instruments. Groups that prepared children for transition to pre-school were popular.

'Getting ready for nursery' group

This transition group boosted parents' and children's confidence in preparing for nursery class or pre-school playgroup. The groups informed parents about listening skills, story-telling and reading books, the foundation stage and the ways parents can support their children's learning. Where crèches were provided, parents gained confidence in leaving their child and realised the need to develop the child's independence. Local teachers collaborated with the SSLP to explain school practices. Some sessions catered for small numbers of children, average age 2 years and 9 months, who needed to develop confidence or whose speech and language needed further assessment.

The routine and discipline of a 'Ready for nursery' group were tough for some parents. Some 3-year-olds were still receiving diets suitable for babies and were regularly offered a feeding bottle. At snack time, the requirement for hand washing surprised many parents, and some found the routines of songs and actions embarrassing. Many depressed or agoraphobic parents were anxious about attending groups but were encouraged and supported by the home visitors who had raised concerns about their child's lack of confidence and language development. These parents often defined their anxiety in terms of 'the child lacking experience of mixing with other children'. However, they often benefited as much as the child.

Only a minority of SSLPs demonstrated commitment to activities promoting literacy. Most included songs with rhyming sounds in their early learning and play sessions. A few understood the importance of rhyme and phonemic awareness. One teacher said: 'Sometimes when I've explained the theoretical reason why we're doing something there's a glazed expression and I have had to think about the language that I use, because education can be full of phrase words and buzz words'.

Another teacher, realising that parents may need guidance in promoting children's learning, said: ' ... Parents are thinking ... "I wonder what happens when they get to school, how will I be able to help them?" [so I arranged a matching game] and said "... matching is one of the first stages of children's reading" and they all went "ahh" in relief and said "Well I can do that, I can help them"'.

Key messages

- By spending time disseminating expertise in language acquisition to SSLP staff trained in other disciplines, SaLTs had more impact than by working with individual children.
- Collaboration between SaLTs, SSLP staff and educators on the ground was generally good, but a lack of a shared philosophy, terminology and conceptual framework related to child development hindered communication between professionals.
- Among generalist staff there were varying abilities to identify children with potentially serious communication problems and disorders.
- Understanding of how to promote pre-literacy skills was limited. Although Bookstart was used in the 15 SSLPs, modelling how to use the books was not universal. Most SSLPs included activities that involved rhyming, but few staff saw their relevance to literacy. Conceptual frameworks (such as ORIM) were not widely disseminated.
- Parents appreciated understanding their role in supporting their children's communication skills.
- There was wide variation in the quality of crèches, day care and group work. Some group activities and day care settings were well run, with coherent plans and programmes, a range of relevant curriculum activities and regular routines. But others lacked routines, were under-staffed, and offered poorly planned and supervised activities to promote speech and language development, with low levels of adult–child interactions.
- There was widespread agreement that more investment is needed in promoting speech and language development where children and their parents are working in a second language.

Conclusion

The findings of the study have implications for Sure Start children's centres:

- SaLTs and appropriately qualified teachers play a vital role in ensuring that emerging knowledge about what works in early language acquisition, and the building blocks of early literacy, is made available to all pre-school children.

- The benefits of a close relationship between SSLP staff and SaLTs were apparent, and sufficient time must be built into SaLT contracts to make this work in children's centres. There is urgency if gains made by SSLPs are to be sustained, as many SaLT contracts with primary care trusts will have to be renewed.
- The introduction in September 2008 of the Early Years Foundation Stage (EYFS), common to all disciplines working with birth to 5-year-old children, will simplify inter-professional communication and collaboration, but will generate extensive staff training needs.
- More could be done to implement recent research on the foundations of literacy.
- Training staff in child development, the identification of children whose development is atypical, and the issue of bilingualism should figure prominently in preparation for the implementation of EYFS curriculum. A debate about structure, routines and parental commitment in pre-school settings needs to be initiated through joint training for professionals from different agencies.
- The task of training children's centre staff is daunting.

Note

1 People who worked for the library service and were brought in wholly or partly by Sure Start had different titles: Early Years Outreach Librarian; Library Links Worker; Early Years Library Worker; Family Literacy Outreach Worker. Although the titles differed, they had similar roles.

References

Bialystok, E. (2001) *Bilingualism in Development: Language, Literacy and Cognition.* New York: Cambridge University Press.

Bishop, D.V.M. (1997) *Uncommon Understanding: Development and Disorders of Language Comprehension in Children.* Hove: Psychology Press.

Brazelton, T.B. and Nugent, J.K. (1995) *Neonatal Behavioural Assessment Scale.* London: MacKeith.

Bronfenbrenner, U. (1979) *The Ecology of Human Development: Experiments by Nature and Design.* Cambridge, MA: Harvard University Press.

Dale, P.S., Simonoff, E., Bishop, D.V.M., Eley, T., Oliver, B., Price, T., Purcell, S., Stevenson, J. and Planin, R. (1998) 'Genetic influence on language delay in two-year-old children', *Nature Neuroscience*, 1, 324–8.

DfES (Department for Education and Skills) (2007) *The Early Years Foundation Stage: Setting the Standards for Learning, Development and Care for Children from Birth to Five.* London: HMSO.

Feinstein, L. (2003) 'Inequality in the early cognitive development of British children in the 1970 cohort', *Economica*, 70, 73–97.

Fey, M.E. (1986) *Language Intervention with Young Children.* San Diego, CA: College-Hill.

Fortnum, H.M., Summerfield, A.Q., Marshall, D.H., Davis, A.C. and Bamford, J.M. (2001) 'Prevalence of permanent childhood hearing impairment in the United Kingdom and implications for universal neonatal hearing screening: questionnaire-based ascertainment study', *British Medical Journal*, 323: 536–40.

Girolametto, L., Weitzman, E. and Greenberg, E. (2003) 'Training day care staff to facilitate children's language', *American Journal of Speech-Language Pathology*, 12(3): 299–311.

Glogowska, M. and Campbell, R. (2004) 'Parental views of surveillance for early speech and language difficulties', *Children and Society*, 18, 266–77.

Goswami, U.C. and Bryant, P. (1990) *Phonological Skills and Learning to Read: Essays in Developmental Psychology*. Hove: Psychology Press.

Hannon, P. (1995) *Literacy, Home and School: Research and Practice in Teaching Literacy with Parents*. London: Falmer.

Hart, B. and Risley, T.R. (1995) *Meaningful Differences in the Everyday Experiences of Young American Children*. Baltimore, MD: Paul Brookes.

Hart, B. and Risley, T.R. (1999) *The Social World of Children Learning to Talk*. Baltimore, MD: Paul Brookes.

Ireton, H. (1990) 'Developmental screening measures', in J.H. Johnson and J. Goldman (eds), *Developmental Assessment in Child Psychology*. New York: Pergamon.

Law, J., Boyle, J., Harris, F., Harkness, A. and Nye, C. (1998) 'Screening for speech and language delay: a systematic review of the literature', *Health Technology Assessment*, 2, 1–184.

Law, J. and Harris, F. (2001) *Promoting Speech and Language Development: Guidance For Sure Start Programmes*. (Available at www.surestart.gov.uk/publications/index. cfm?document=753)

Mahoney, G. and MacDonald, J. (2004) *Responsive Teaching: Parent Mediated Developmental Intervention – Intervention Components and Procedures*. Cleveland, OH: Case Western University, Mandel School of Applied Sciences.

McLoyd, V. (1998) 'Socioeconomic disadvantage and child development', *American Psychologist*, 53, 185–204.

Meisels, S.J. and Atkins-Burnett, S. (2000) 'Elements of early childhood assessment', in J.P. Shonkoff and S.J. Meisels (eds), *Handbook of Early Childhood Intervention*. Cambridge: Cambridge University Press.

Moore, M. and Wade, B. (2003) 'Bookstart: a qualitative evaluation', *Educational Review*, 55, 3–13.

Nutbrown, C., Hannon, P. and Morgan, M. (2005) *Early Literacy Work with Families: Policy, Practice and Research*. London: Sage.

Royal College of Speech and Language Therapists (2006) *Communicating Quality 3: RCSLTs Best Guidance in Service Organisation and Delivery*. London: Royal College of Speech and Language Therapists.

Rutter, M.L. (1999) 'Psychosocial adversity and child psychopathology (Review article)', *The British Journal of Psychiatry*, 174, 480–93.

Sawyer, V., Pickstone, C. and Hall, D. (2007) *Speech and Language Services in Sure Start Local Programmes. Report 22*. Nottingham: Department for Education and Skills.

Schweinhart, L.J., Barnes, H. and Weikart, D. (eds) (1993) *Significant Benefits: The High/Scope Perry Pre-school Study Through Age 27*. Ypsilanti, MI: High/Scope.

Tallal, P. and Benasich, A.A. (2002) 'Developmental language learning environments', *Development and Psychopathology*, 14: 559–79.

Webster Stratton, C. and Mostyn, D. (1992) *Incredible Years: Trouble-shooting Guide for Parents and Children Aged 3–8*. Toronto: Umbrella Press.

Suggested further reading

Evangelou, M. and Sylva, K. (2003) *The Effects of the Peers Early Educational Partnership (PEEP) on Children's Developmental Progress*. Nottingham: DfES.

Nutbrown, C., Hannon, P. and Morgan, M. (2005) *Early Literacy Work With Families: Policy Practice and Research*. London: Sage.

9 Improving the Employability of Parents

Pamela Meadows

This chapter:

- discusses policy and practice in promoting parental employment
- describes five approaches adopted by Sure Start Local Programmes (SSLPs) to address employability
- examines some processes of SSLP employment services and their outcomes
- explores implications for children's centres.

Key questions:

- How have changes in family lives impacted on employment patterns in the UK?
- How did SSLPs address employability targets in so-called disadvantaged areas?
- What problems did they encounter and how did they tackle them?
- What lessons can be learned for children's centres?

Employing parents

Employability is the ability to gain and keep a job, and to cope with changing employment conditions both in the workplace and in the wider economy, including the ability to get a new job if necessary. It includes knowledge and skills, how these are deployed, how they are presented to employers and the personal circumstances and labour market environment within which an individual is operating (Hillage and Pollard, 1998). Measures to improve employability can operate on any one of these elements.

On average nearly half the children aged 0–3 living in Sure Start local programme areas lived in households where no adult had a job. Reducing this share by promoting the employability of parents was one of the four core Sure Start service targets for the period 2003–04 to 2005–06. However, when the first Sure Start local programmes were established this was not part of their remit.

There are two broad reasons for promoting parents' employability. The first is that parental employment has a direct and immediate impact on family incomes. At the time of the Sure Start intervention, the introduction of the more generous Working Families Tax Credit (now Working Tax Credit) replaced previous in-work benefits such as Family Credit. Families with an adult working a minimum of 16 hours a week were generally at least £50 a week better off than they would have been with no working adult. Getting a job is the most effective route out of poverty, although this is not true for all families. Larger families and those living in areas with high childcare costs or rents are not always better off if they take paid work, but for most it makes a large difference to their incomes.

But there is a second reason to promote paid employment for adults: it promotes social integration. There is evidence that children with employed parents make better progress at school, and therefore the children themselves have better earnings potential as they move into adulthood (see, for example, Feinstein, 1998; Ermisch et al., 2001; Gregg et al., 1999). Thus, improving parental employability is part of the process of investing in children's long-term future.

There is also a third reason. Absence from paid employment for childrearing has a detrimental effect on the lifetime incomes of mothers. The penalty is particularly marked for mothers with few or no qualifications and may be at least £250,000 for those with two children (Joshi, 2002; Rake, 2000).

The employability study

Most of the programmes in the themed study on employability (Meadows and Garbers, 2004) were chosen because their spending or their literature suggested that they had activities which addressed the employability target. They were therefore drawn from the more committed end of the SSLP spectrum. Nevertheless, with the exception of the programmes in the active group, programme managers and staff were often ambivalent about the desirability of the target and less than enthusiastic in their pursuit of it. Many argued that their focus was on the welfare of the children and believed that this was not best served by encouraging mothers to engage in paid work.

The study was undertaken during 2003. It was based on 25 case studies of SSLP activities which were aimed at addressing the employability target, summarised (anonymously) in Table 9.1. The original aim of the study was to focus on the activities of SSLPs which were operating in areas with high rates of children living in workless households (although this was later relaxed to include areas with lower worklessness rates). A second aim was to have a range of labour market conditions as some programmes had high proportions of children living in workless households in spite of being in areas where the labour market generally was quite strong.

What did SSLP employability services look like?

The approaches adopted by the 25 SSLPs in the study fell into five broad groups defined as active, lifelong learning, quasi-intermediate labour market (quasi-ILM), passive and disengaged. The groupings were based on the nature of the services that the programmes themselves provided for parents who might want to find work, and also on the extent and nature of their engagement with other organisations providing appropriate services.

Active programmes

One-third of the programmes in the study (eight) were identified as being active. They were distinguished by the enthusiastic approach they took to

Table 9.1   Characteristics of case study programmes

Region	% children aged 0–3 in workless households[1]	% local unemployment rate[2]	% ethnic minority[3]	% of population qualified to A-level or above[4]	Group
East Midlands	60–69	10–14.9	5–24	30.6	Passive
North West	70–79	10–14.9	5–24	25.9	Active
South West	50–59	5–9.9	<5	26.1	Active
North West	70–79	20+	<5	24.4	Disengaged
North East	60–69	15–19.9	25–49	47.0	Active
South West	50–59	10–14.9	<5	22.7	Active
Yorkshire & the Humber	60–69	15–19.9	<5	21.3	Lifelong learning
East	<40	<5	<5	35.5	Disengaged
Yorkshire & the Humber	50–59	15–19.9	<5	21.4	Active
North East	40–49	5–9.9	<5	30.7	Lifelong learning
London	50–59	5–9.9	25–49	59.3	Lifelong Learning
West Midlands	50–59	15–19.9	>50	31.2	Passive
London	<40	5–9.9	25–49	44.7	Lifelong learning
East Midlands	<40	5–9.9	<5	35.3	Lifelong learning
North West	<40	5–9.9	25–49	32.0	Active
South East	40–49	5–9.9	25–49	52.7	Quasi-ILM
London	60–69	10–14.9	>50	45.5	Active
Yorkshire & the Humber	50–59	10–14.9	<5	22.7	Quasi-ILM
London	40–49	5–9.9	25–49	39.7	Passive
Yorkshire & the Humber	50–59	15–19.9	25–49	35.0	Lifelong learning
North West	60–69	10–14.9	<5	24.6	Passive
Yorkshire & the Humber	50–59	10–14.9	<5	23.4	Disengaged
London	50–59	15–19.9	25–49	36.8	Passive
North West	80+	20+	25–49	40.1	Disengaged
North West	70–79	15–19.9	5–24	41.5	Active

Notes:

1. Children in workless households based on Department for Work and Pensions counts April 2003 and 2001 of children dependent on at least one of Job Seekers Allowance, Income Support, Incapacity Benefit, or Severe Disablement Allowance.

Table 9.1   *(Continued)*

2. Local unemployment rate based on Census 2001, Table CAS021, Number unemployed aged 16 to 74 economically active/number all people aged 16 to 74 economically active.
3. Ethnic minority proportion based on Census 2001, Table KS06, percentage non-white.
4. Qualified to A-level and above based on Census 2001, Table CAS105, Number of all people aged 16 to 74 with at least one A-level or above /All people aged 16 to 74.

Source: Meadows and Garbers, 2004: 8–10.

helping parents find work, and by their commitment to this objective. They saw helping parents to find work as important in terms of developing the parents' confidence and empowering them in their wider lives.

Characteristics of active SSLPs

Active SSLPs recognised that the barriers to work facing parents living in Sure Start areas are often complicated. Some have never worked since leaving school. Many had poor experiences at school and have few qualifications. Their confidence levels are low. They are worried about managing their money when they go into work, while on benefits their key bills such as rent are taken care of. They have transport problems. They need suitable and affordable childcare for their children under four, but they often have older children with childcare needs too. Active programmes recognised that it was not enough to tackle any one of these issues in isolation, since each could be enough in itself to prevent a parent from finding and keeping work. They therefore put services in place, either directly, or via referrals to other agencies, that helped parents to sort out each of the problems.

Most of the active programmes worked closely with regeneration initiatives which were operating in their areas. Some of them had shared boundaries with other initiatives, and sometimes they came under a common management umbrella. All the staff in active programmes, not just those engaged in employment and training work, could offer parents advice and support on employment-related issues, and could signpost them to appropriate services.

Lifelong learning programmes

A quarter of the SSLPs (six) emphasised the importance of encouraging parents to gain new skills. These programmes were similar in many ways to the active programmes.

However, there was less support or encouragement for parents who wanted to take up employment immediately. Links with colleges and other training providers were good, but links with employment schemes and with Jobcentre Plus were often weak.

Characteristics of lifelong learning SSLPs

In lifelong learning SSLPs staff were enthusiastic, encouraging and well informed. However, the emphasis was on ensuring that parents would be in a position to move into work later when their children were at primary school rather than into immediate employment. They offered a large menu of training opportunities, some child-related (such as child protection, child behaviour management and baby massage), some just aiming to attract people back to learning (such as salsa, nail painting and aromatherapy) and some focusing on general skills (such as literacy, English language or information technology). Finally, they supported people who wanted to build on what they had learned and to develop advanced skills at National Vocational Qualifications (NVQ), III up to degree and professional qualification level.

Quasi-ILM programmes

Two of the SSLPs took a more radical approach. Their starting point was that Sure Start brought resources and jobs into the area. Providing jobs within the programme itself for local people was an important way of improving the income levels within the community, and of developing the skill base. These programmes were essentially using the programme itself as an intermediate labour market for local people, providing paid work experience in a supportive environment.

Characteristics of quasi-intermediate labour market SSLPs

Quasi-ILM programmes took the services for children and families that the programme would be delivering and structured the jobs needed to deliver them in a way that would maximise the chance that local people, particularly parents, would be able to take them. Thus, although some jobs might require full-time work and professional qualifications, many would not. In order to improve the employment chances of parents and other local people, the programmes offered pre-recruitment training in how to apply for the jobs and had negotiated exemption from the parent body's equal opportunities policy in order to do so. Programme staff were given the opportunity to develop a range of skills, including accredited qualifications, which would enable them to move on to other work in due course.

Passive programmes

There were five SSLPs which appeared to have many of the same links and opportunities that lifelong learning and active programmes had. However, although they provided signposting to colleges, training providers and employment opportunities, they did not actively encourage or promote the opportunities available.

Disengaged programmes

The four SSLPs in the disengaged group did not have many links with employment or training providers, and offered little by way of signposting to parents. Essentially, they were ignoring the employability target.

Working with and through other agencies

Sure Start local programmes worked towards their employability target by working with organisations with expertise in the field. The success or otherwise of a particular collaboration did not seem to depend on the contractual form of the relationship. Some successful collaborations operated in an environment of strict service-level agreement contracts between the SSLP and its partners, while others operated on a much more informal give-and-take basis. The attitudes of those involved, a sense of shared purpose and a willingness to be flexible characterised most of the successful relationships.

Where regeneration initiatives such as the New Deal for Communities were operating, some programmes engaged in active collaboration, while others had no links at all. Relationships with colleges were also mixed. Some were genuinely collaborative with commitment on both sides and a recognition that there were mutual advantages to working together. Where SSLPs succeeded in getting parents actively engaged in learning they could become an important potential client group for the college's own provision and enable less popular courses to become viable. In other cases, however, SSLPs found that colleges were unwilling to change the nature or location of their provision to suit the needs of parents with young children, or to provide crèches.

The provision of childcare while parents were taking part in training courses emerged as essential. Most of the Sure Start local programmes included in the study were providing crèches or childminders for parents doing courses organised by the SSLPs themselves (and sometimes for other training courses as well). Where childcare was limited or not available, parents generally found it difficult to undertake training.

Relationships with Jobcentre Plus were limited. Most programmes worked closely with benefits advisers, and those in areas where Action Teams for Jobs were operating collaborated with them. Otherwise links were mainly confined to those operating through multi-agency collaborations rather than directly with Jobcentres themselves. Part of the reason for this was that parents who were benefit recipients often had an uneasy relationship with Jobcentre Plus, and the SSLPs were unwilling to be seen to be collaborating with them too closely.

Employment and training co-ordinators

The active and lifelong learning programmes were distinguished by their employment of staff whose role was to act as a bridge between parents and other service providers, and to provide individual advice and support for parents. These people helped parents access training and job opportunities, and encouraged employers and education and training providers to remove unnecessary barriers.

In lifelong learning programmes the people doing this kind of work were generally called training co-ordinators, and their job was to develop the training directories and to organise all the training SSLPs offer to parents, volunteers and board members. They also negotiated with external providers and helped Sure Start parents to access mainstream provision, including helping them with childcare.

Benefits advisers

Many SSLPs found that a fundamental prerequisite to successfully facilitating parents' movement into employment was the availability of a benefits adviser. SSLPs often arranged for a Jobcentre Plus benefits adviser to have a regular drop-in session in the Sure Start centre. Sometimes benefits advice was provided by an independent agency such as the Citizens' Advice Bureau. The advisers were able to calculate for parents their potential entitlement to in-work support were they to start work including Working Families Tax Credit (now Working Tax Credit) and housing benefit.

Engagement of parents

Confidence-building plays an important role in bringing parents to the point where they are able to start developing new skills. Almost all the SSLPs in the study reported that it was often difficult to engage mothers' interest in employment or training activities; as argued throughout the book fathers were rarely in touch with the programmes. Few wanted paid work until their children were at primary school. As part of this study interviews were held with 58 parents (who were generally drawn from the minority who were already interested in employment and training), which confirmed this.

This is consistent with the general working pattern of mothers in Britain. Only around half of all mothers of children under five are in paid employment, and the majority of those are working part-time. However, employment rates tend to rise rapidly once children are in school.

Overall, even in the most active programmes, fewer than one in ten parents were engaged in any form of activity that related to improving employability, and only around one in ten of these was interested in immediate employment. Learner groups of fewer than ten were common, especially for more vocational courses, and programmes were pleased where they had groups of 15 or more. As a consequence employment advisers, where they were employed by programmes, had very small case loads (sometimes in single figures).

To the extent that parents had an interest in immediate paid work, they generally wanted part-time jobs that they could fit around their families, rather than setting up arrangements for their families which enabled them to take particular jobs. This is in line with previous research which suggests that this is the preferred approach of women whose primary focus is on their role as mothers (Hakim, 1996; Marsh et al., 2001; Millar and Ridge, 2001).

Active programmes took the view that part of their responsibility was to challenge any reluctance on the part of parents to take paid employment, and that paid employment was a route not only to higher family incomes, but also to increased confidence and greater ability to manage all aspects of their lives. They believed that the choice not to engage in paid employment was not necessarily in parents' own best interests.

Childcare

Only a minority of the 25 case study programmes were providing childcare for working parents, or had any plans to do so. Those that did were typically offering around 30 places, almost all for children over two. The demand from parents for formal full-time childcare was low. Many parents were reluctant to use non-family childcare on a regular basis (although crèche sessions both for respite and while parents were doing training courses were popular: see Chapter 7). Other research has found the same (Ford, 1996; Woodland et al., 2002; Himmelweit and Sigala, 2004; Dex, 2003).

One of the reasons for the limited demand for childcare is that even with the childcare element of the Working Tax Credit, childcare for children under school age is expensive. In 2007 the typical (unsubsidised) cost in England of a full-time nursery place for a child under two is £152 a week. In London it is typically £205 a week (Daycare Trust 2007). The childcare element of the Working Tax Credit is worth up to 80 per cent of eligible childcare costs (£175 a week for one child, £300 a week for two or more children) depending on the family's income. But at a minimum, parents have to pay 20 per cent of their childcare costs and most pay more.

Only one programme in the study had placed a high priority on subsidising childcare for parents who were working. The provision was very welcome to those parents who were using it, but there were fewer than 30 places, and the cost to the programme of the subsidy was £175,000 a year or around £110 per place per week. This would not be a viable option for the long term.

Measuring outcomes

Given the small number of parents taking part in employment and vocational training activities, few programmes were formally monitoring achieved outcomes. Almost all the more active programmes had stories of people who had started on confidence-building courses and had gone on to qualify at NVQ III or were studying to degree level. Most programmes had parents whom they had trained as parents' forum members, as board members or as volunteers who had gone on to use the skills and confidence they had gained from the experience to take up paid employment (although a few felt that this meant that the training had been 'wasted').

However, the approach adopted by programmes in the three active groups (active, lifelong learning and quasi-ILM) was in line with research-evidence about what works in terms of helping people from disadvantaged groups or lone parents equip themselves for work (see, for example, Campbell and Meadows, 2001; Evans et al., 2003). Moreover, the personalised approach and the very small caseloads reinforce the likelihood that the efforts involved are likely to have positive outcomes.

Conclusion

The *Sure Start Children's Centres Practice Guidance* (DfES 2005) required them to offer opportunities to promote parents' interests in work-related skills and access to e-learning opportunities; to help unemployed parents to find work (linking with Jobcentre Plus and local employers); and to provide childcare for working parents and for those attending education or training sessions. In responding to the guidance, what can Sure Start children's centres learn from the experience of SSLPs?

Many SSLPs expressed some ambivalence about the appropriateness of an employability target. Parents themselves are often reluctant, for both cultural and financial reasons, to take paid work before their children are at primary school. Yet paid work is the main route out of poverty and its associated disadvantages.

By emphasising confidence-building, raising aspirations, and helping parents to improve their skills, Sure Start children's centres can reconcile any potential conflict between promoting good parenting and promoting employability. They can provide parents with greater control over their lives and greater choice about how and when to engage with paid work. Moreover, parents who have learnt new skills are likely to have access to a greater range of job opportunities than those who go straight into paid work. The model of SSLPs taking a lifelong learning approach is useful in that it challenges parents' reluctance to learn and develop their skills, and allows them to make up their own minds about the value of immediate paid work.

References

Campbell, M. and Meadows, P. (2001) *What Works Locally? Key Lessons on Local Employment Policies*. York: York Publishing Services.

Daycare Trust (2007) *Childcare Costs 2007*.
(*Available at* www.daycaretrust.org.uk/mod.php?mod=userpage&menu=1003&page_id=226)

Dex, S. (2003) *Families and Work in the Twenty-first Century*. York: Joseph Rowntree Foundation.

DfES (Department for Education and Skills) (2005) *Sure Start Children's Centre Practice Guidance*. London: DfES.

Ermisch, J., Francesconi, M. and Pevalin, D.J. (2001) *Outcomes for Children of Poverty*, Report no 158. London: Department for Work and Pensions Research.

Evans, M., Eyre, J., Millar, J. and Sarre, S. (2003). *New Deal for Lone Parents: Second Synthesis Report of the National Evaluation*, Working Age Research and Analysis Report no 163. London: Department for Work and Pensions.

Feinstein, L. (1998) *Pre-school Educational Inequality? British Children in the 1970 Cohort*, Centre for Economic Performance Discussion Paper no 404. London: London School of Economics.

Ford, R. (1996) *Childcare in the Balance: How Lone Parents Make Decisions about Work*. York: York Publishing Services.

Gregg, P., Harkness, S. and Machin, S. (1999) *Child Development and Family Income*. York: York Publishing Services.

Hakim, C. (1996) *Female Heterogeneity and the Polarisation of Women's Employment*. London: Athlone Press.

Hillage, J. and Pollard, E. (1998) *Employability: Developing a Framework for Policy Analysis*, Report RR85. London: Department for Education and Employment Research.

Himmelweit, S. and Sigala, M. (2004) 'Choice and the relationship between identities and behaviour for mothers with pre-school children: some implications for policy from a UK study', *Journal of Social Policy*, 33(3): 455–78.

Joshi, H. (2002) 'Production, reproduction, and education: women, children, and work in a British perspective', *Population and Development Review*, 28(3): 445–74.

Marsh, A., McKay, S., Smith, A. and Stephenson, A. (2001) *Low-Income Families in Britain: Work, Welfare and Social Security in 1999*, Department of Social Security Research Report No 138. Leeds: Corporate Document Services.

Meadows, P. and Garbers, C. (2004) *Sure Start Local Programmes: Improving the Employability of Parents*, National Evaluation of Sure Start. Nottingham: Department for Education and Skills.

Millar, J. and Ridge, T. (2001) *Families, Poverty, Work and Care: A Review of the Literature on Lone Parents and Low Income Couple Families*, Department of Social Security Research Report no 153. Leeds: Corporate Document Services.

Rake, K. (ed.) (2000) *Women's Incomes over the Lifetime: Report for the Women's Unit, Cabinet Office*. London: The Stationery Office.

Woodland, S., Miller, M. and Tipping, S. (2002) *Repeat Study of Parents' Demand for Childcare*, Research Report No. 348. London: Department for Education and Skills.

Suggested further reading

Dex, S. (2003) *Families and Work in the Twenty-first Century*. York: Joseph Rowntree Foundation.

Ford, R. (1996) *Childcare in the Balance: How Lone Parents Make Decisions about Work*. York: York Publishing Services.

Meadows, P. and Garbers, C. (2004) *Sure Start Local Programmes: Improving the Employability of Parents* National Evaluation of Sure Start. Nottingham: Department for Education and Skills.

Millar, J. and Ridge, T. (2001) *Families, Poverty, Work and Care: A Review of the Literature on Lone Parents and Low Income Couple Families*, Department of Social Security Research Report no 153. Leeds: Corporate Document Services.

Part 4

Safeguarding and Promoting the Welfare of Children

Sharing Information

Working with children and families, satisfying and exhilarating though it may be, brings with it some weighty and burdensome dilemmas. All practitioners will be equipped by their training to understand their statutory responsibilities and duties to children at risk. The advantage of the Sure Start approach was that the weighty elements of the work could be shared with colleagues, making it less likely that a worker would feel isolated (and make hasty decisions as a result) and less likely that families will drop through the net. Nevertheless, robust line management and supervisory systems had to be in place to ensure that correct procedures were always carried out.

One of the successes of Sure Start was that its services were not stigmatised as being directed at the poor and disadvantaged – they were seen as universal. Maintaining the spirit of openness and attractiveness is important, but in that context professionals still have to adhere to protocols which protect children. These will include both sharing information accurately and appropriately and protecting information when it needs confidential treatment. The common assessment framework

(CAF) provides the basis for handling sensitive cases. Stigma can be avoided where the statutory services are bedded in a context of universal provision. The same principle has allowed children with special needs and disabilities to benefit from mainstream provision and targeted services.

10 Parenting Support in Sure Start

Jane Barlow, Sue Kirkpatrick and Sarah Stewart-Brown

This chapter:

- describes the association between the sort of parenting that a child receives and his or her likelihood of social exclusion later in life
- examines the evidence about 'what works' in terms of parenting support
- explores variations in family/parent and parenting support across Sure Start Local Programmes (SSLPs)
- discusses evidence of impact and implications for practice

Key questions:

- o Why can it be difficult to get parenting support to those families who may benefit from it most?
- o What other kinds of support can help disadvantaged families with their parenting role besides parenting education?
- o What kinds of attitudes are required in practitioners who are delivering parenting support programmes?

Background

There is strong research evidence to associate parenting with a range of outcomes that are linked with social exclusion, and that influence a child's likelihood of later educational and economic success. Such evidence has buttressed the provision of support to disadvantaged parents and families both nationally and internationally, particularly during the first five years of a child's life.

As part of the effort to support disadvantaged families, Sure Start Local Programmes (SSLPs) aimed to reduce social exclusion by reducing poverty (helping parents to get back to work) and by supporting parents and the family more generally. Early findings from the National Evaluation of Sure Start (NESS) suggest that while the overall programme had limited impact (NESS, 2005a; Belsky et al., 2006), local programmes that were better led, with clearer objectives, and which used effective methods of identifying families, produced better outcomes (NESS, 2005b; Melhuish et al., 2007).

Given the link between parenting and later outcomes it seemed pertinent to examine whether the provision of parenting support within Sure Start could be linked to programme effectiveness. This chapter therefore explores these early findings from the National Evaluation in the light of data obtained from a survey examining the nature and extent of parenting support in Sure Start (Barlow et al., 2007).

The issues: parenting and social exclusion

From its election in 1997, the Labour Government emphasised the need to tackle a range of problems including obesity, alcohol and drug abuse, teenage pregnancy, smoking, delinquency, mental health problems, exercise and eating patterns and so on (DoH, 2004). These issues were recognised to be associated with social exclusion, thereby limiting opportunity for those on the margins.

Social inequality has a detrimental effect on child development (Brooks-Gunn and Duncan, 1997), indicating a need for initiatives to reduce childhood poverty. However, there is also accumulating evidence that parenting is a mediator of the effect of socio-economic deprivation in childhood on outcomes in later life (for example, Conger et al., 1992; Zaslow et al., 1985; Belsky et al., 2006). Combined with research showing that improvement in the financial circumstances of deprived parents does not, on its own, improve parenting or child development, this pointed to a need for parenting support to be an essential companion to initiatives to reduce childhood poverty (Bos et al., 1999; Morris and Michalopoulos, 2000).

The sort of parenting a child receives is also associated with their likelihood of educational achievement and of school drop-out (Desforges, 2003); the occurrence of behaviour problems, delinquency, criminality and violence (Patterson et al., 1989; Farrington, 2003); teenage pregnancy (Scaramella et al., 1998); drug and alcohol misuse (Egland et al., 1993); and mental and physical health (Stewart-Brown and Shaw, 2004). This is because parenting is strongly associated with a range of shorter term outcomes such as attachment security, self-esteem, emotional regulation, capacity for communication and relationships. These in turn influence the likelihood of a child developing behaviour problems, school failure, delinquency, sexual promiscuity, smoking and drug abuse.

Supporting parenting: what works?

There is a large body of evidence – at least five systematic reviews – (Tennant et al., 2007) – showing that the provision of parenting support at important key stages of a child's development is an effective way of improving outcomes for children (for example, Bakermans-Kranenburg et al., 1998; Barnes and Freude-Lagevardi, 2003; Moran et al., 2004; Dretzke et al., 2005; and Barlow et al., 2005). Collectively, this evidence provides substantial support for the use of a range of parenting interventions that begin during the antenatal period and continue throughout infancy and early childhood, including parenting (mostly behavioural) and intensive home visiting programmes, in addition to a range of innovative perinatal programmes (mostly attachment based) and early learning programmes (see Barlow et al., 2007 for further detail). What most of these interventions have in common, irrespective of the age of the child, is that they provide formalised ways to support parenting skills, often by providing additional skills, insight or understanding in terms of the parent's relationship with their child, and ways of parenting.

In addition, these reviews suggest that:

- manualised programmes with centrally-monitored, systematised delivery tend to deliver better outcomes;
- programme integrity matters;
- quality and training of staff is vital to programme success;

- programmes that do not pay close attention to implementation factors are unlikely to be successful;
- successful programmes address more than one area of need, without losing sight of their core objectives;
- interventions that involve children as well as parents show better outcomes.

This evidence provided clear lessons for Sure Start. However, the wide variety of ways of working with parents described in guidance for Sure Start programmes may have prevented these lessons being used locally to ensure success.

Sure start: the model

The initial guidance for Sure Start emphasised a 'bottom-up' approach intended to empower the local community which, together with a reluctance to specify models or protocols, offered SSLPs a high degree of autonomy and ensured a wide variety of provision. Thus, while providing support for families was a core requirement, there were no explicit requirements in terms of the type of support to be provided.

The broader goal underpinning Sure Start was to break the cycle of disadvantage by improving outcomes for parents and children, and more specifically by improving the health, education and emotional development of young children. Employment opportunities for parents and childcare were the two central planks of this strategy, thereby tackling poverty head on.

However, emerging evidence suggested that reducing poverty alone would not improve outcomes for young children, without services aimed explicitly at supporting parenting (for example, Bos et al., 1999; Morris and Michalopoulos, 2000). Consensus showed that interventions worked best when they balanced central direction on the requirements for effective service provision, with room for programmes to innovate locally.

Sure Start directives made no distinction between services to support parents and families, and those to support parenting more directly, and there was no direction given about the balance between the two. There was some limited guidance about 'what works'. Combined with a very powerful rhetoric about empowering parents, and user-led service provision, the stage was set for what was later to emerge from the National Evaluation.

Parenting support in Sure Start

Toward the end of 2005 an independent survey (Barlow et al., 2007) examined the nature and extent of parenting support in Sure Start. This showed that a majority (that is, two-thirds) of the support being provided could be classified as *parenting support* (including parenting programmes; home visiting/outreach; perinatal programmes; and early learning) the remainder being *family/parent support*. This suggests that SSLPs clearly recognised the need to provide explicit support for parenting. However, a closer look at the ways in which the support was being provided suggested inadequacies in the light of what research had shown to be good practice.

Thus, while most of the support being provided would be classified as aimed at supporting parenting, there were few standardised evidence-based programmes or use of manuals to guide provision, little evidence of staff having received additional training or ongoing supervision to support parenting, and considerable evidence of improvisation in the sense of staff putting things together from the bottom up. One member of staff expressed this as follows:

'The programme that we came across in America years and years ago was brought over [...] by a head teacher that went on a study tour and we sort of looked at it and we thought it has got some potential but it was a long way off what we wanted at the time. So we developed it from there.' (Family support worker, SSLP; Barlow et al., 2007: 23)

Many SSLPs developed programmes locally and delivered them to groups of parents. Such programmes comprised a mixture of components:

'The material is put together by different members of staff who work within the programme. So there might be something that looks at play with babies and that might be delivered by one of the early learning staff. There might be a session with language support and that might be delivered by our speech and language therapist. There might be a session on dieting, weaning with particular-aged children and that might be delivered by the dietician. But they are delivered by different members of, you know, the multi-disciplinary team and there may be specialist input. But it is not a package off the shelf. I think the view is that it is informal, it can be a drop-in, but there is a programme of events. The parents will be given the programme and they may choose to attend some of those that might be what they are interested in or more appropriate to their needs. They might have those but they don't necessarily have to attend every single one.' (Manager, SSLP; Barlow et al., 2007: 23)

Use of more innovative methods of supporting parenting during pregnancy and the immediate postnatal period (that is, perinatal programmes) was rare, despite increasing awareness of the need to promote 'sensitive' parenting during the first two years of life. Support during this period was usually delivered by midwives and health visitors and focused predominantly on traditional parent-craft classes, antenatal preparation, breast-feeding advice, and the identification and treatment of post-natal depression. Programmes explicitly aimed at the emotional preparation of parents for parenthood, or that focused on the relationship between mother and baby with a view to promoting a healthy relationship and secure attachment, were on the whole limited to the provision of infant massage classes.

Bottom-up approaches and scepticism on the ground

A finding in many of the SSLPs surveyed was that SSLP staff held very firm views about the appropriateness of certain forms of working with parents (particularly the use of standardised evidence-based programmes). These views were often justified by reference to the original Sure Start guidance and the need for bottom-up and 'needs-led' approaches.

Many staff believed that nationally recognised, structured programmes would not be suitable for families in their localities, with some SSLPs not offering them at all, and others 'screening' parents and dissuading them from taking part. Such feelings about formalised methods of supporting parenting were underpinned by a more far-reaching scepticism about programmes that had not been developed locally, and the use of a 'needs-led' philosophy to obviate the value of such programmes. For example, a staff member described the home visiting situation as follows:

'It depends what the needs are, what have been the flagged-up needs. It is supposed to be a valued added service. So that means sometimes it could be anything – weaning is a favourite one, problems with eating, sleeping, weaning, speech and language; and quite often you find when you when you go in for something, and at that reason to go in, you find that there are other issues that usually women want to deal with. And it may be domestic violence, there are a lot of domestic violence issues in the area – and I think it is getting worse.' (Staff member, SSLP; Barlow et al., 2007: 24)

This description demonstrates a confusion between services that are structured in terms of what is provided but also flexible and responsive, and services that have no structure, clear philosophy or plan in terms of the content of the visits or the methods of working with parents.

SSLP staff expressed the view that parents did not want to attend formal parenting courses and that there was no demand for them:

'I think one of the key things I would have to say in terms of parenting and any with that sort of provision I do think you need a menu of things available to meet different needs. **Because the courses don't do it for the vast majority – courses don't you know.** People are either not going to turn up or that message doesn't work or it might work in a way but it needs supporting by other things.' (Barlow et al., 2007: 22)

Some staff considered the materials in standardised programmes as unsuited to the needs of Sure Start families:

'Briefly quite a long time ago we looked at that material but what was felt was that it was quite jargonistic and **there was a lot of material that we weren't sure that the parents that we were going to invite to come on a course would understand**. It was quite you know – it was more appropriate to professionals than the parents in a Sure Start area.' (Barlow et al., 2007: 22)

Other staff felt that Sure Start parents would not 'stay the course':

'Well 12 weeks is quite a long time for families to keep a programme and the programme is quite lengthy – each session is quite lengthy as well. **And you know to that extent we find it very difficult to commit – to get parents to commit with that kind of intensity really.'** (Barlow et al., 2007: 22)

These views tended to be based on assumptions about parenting programmes rather than the experience of providing such programmes. They contrasted with the attitude of staff in a small number of SSLPs that were providing a range of evidence-based programmes, on a rolling basis, with evidence of good uptake and good attendance on the part of parents. They contrasted too with the views of parents interviewed in those areas, who said that parenting groups provided a safe space to discuss parenting issues without discomfort:

> 'When we do come to this group you can say your child's worst behaviour and also feel comfortable talking about it because you want help for it. And everybody will say you could do this, you could do that and you have got all these ideas in front of you. So it is really good.' (Parent, SSLP case study; Barlow et al., 2007: 49)

Most of the parents who had attended parenting courses had gained new confidence to parent their children differently. Parents described learning new strategies and techniques that they felt enabled them to enhance their parenting and gain a greater sense of control: 'It's something I will always remember, I don't want to be the mum that's screaming constantly. I found I was a lot calmer with her and more patient because I know how to handle her' (Parent, SSLP case study; Barlow et al., 2007: 49).

Structured courses were valued by parents because they provided clear guidelines and some element of predictability: '... this week we are going to do this, this week we will do that. And you know what to expect and it is a very comfortable atmosphere and you get to know a lot of other parents as well. Just knowing so many other parents makes it more comfortable to live in the area' (Parent, SSLP case study; Barlow et al., 2007: 49). This testimony was consistent with that of other parents who have been interviewed following their participation in a standardised parenting programme (Barlow and Stewart-Brown, 2000).

Good practice in Sure Start

So what might an innovative and evidence-based approach to supporting parenting within Sure Start have looked like?

Using a model of change

An essential aspect of good practice was the use of a specific model of change or theoretical approach as the basis on which all staff in Sure Start worked with parents to achieve change. The Solihull approach is an integrated model based on three theories about relating and change – psychoanalytic theory, child developmental theory and behaviourism. The central tenet of this model is that through the development of a reciprocal relationship, an individual can experience emotional containment that supports their capacity to think or manage their own and their children's behaviour. A key feature of the Solihull approach is the concept of 'parallel process' in which all staff 'model' the quality of relationship which can promote emotional containment, and parents can begin to internalise this relationship dynamic and demonstrate it with their children:

> 'What we do is grounded in really good theoretical understanding, so none of us is trying to reinvent the wheel. We're actually trying to do things that we know are effective ... how we think about children playing, adults learning ... people's emotional lives and relationships. It's grounded in a really good theoretical understanding, and that's what makes it work.' (Member of staff, SSLP; Barlow et al., 2007: 36)

Team members were appointed on the basis of their experience and expertise and also on their willingness to contribute to a common vision for the whole team.

Total focus on improving the parent–child relationship

A second aspect was the focus in all aspects of the SSLP on improving the relationship between parents and children. One member of staff said:

> 'Everything we do is ultimately aimed at influencing the way in which parents parent, every single thing from the minute they [parents] walk through the door hopefully, in the way that we are, the way we talk with parents, and the way that we talk with their children ...' (Barlow et al., 2007: 34)

In SSLPs using this approach, interventions directed at supporting parents were also used to support parenting. For example, one centre was providing formal courses in confidence-building and personal development training to help parents become emotionally literate and self-aware by focusing on their own experiences of being parented, and helping them to become aware of the way in which this has impacted on their own parenting:

> 'For me it was a case of seeing things that my mum used to say to me that really kind of brought you down, down, down. It relates back to the positive parenting course I attended – having the positiveness in your children, praising your children.' (Parent, case study; Barlow et al., 2007: 47)

Regular programme provision

The regular provision of at least one evidence-based standardised parenting programme is another important component of good practice. There was a range of examples of good practice with regard to the use of standardised programmes, particularly in terms of the recruitment and retention of parents (see Barlow et al., 2007 for further detail).

Long-term active support

Providing active support for parenting from pregnancy through to toddlerhood and beyond has also been implemented, using innovative methods of working with parents. Some examples are given below.

Antenatal support

One programme manager told us:

'The midwife runs a group for parents-to-be...although she does talk about labour and all the things that parents are interested in, **the emphasis all the time is on the growing relationship between the parent-to-be and their baby, and how it changes, the dynamics of the household, and all of that**. And it is delivered by the midwife but we always have a child psychotherapist or our CPN in that group. So what we are trying to do is all the time from the outset – get away from the idea that the baby is a package that they do something unto ... but trying to develop the idea that it is the relationships that will decide how that baby is ...' (Barlow et al., 2007: 42)

For parents with young babies

Tuning into Babies is a programme in which parents attend a 2-hour group session of structured activities where they learn about communication with babies. They are encouraged to think about their baby as a social being and to become aware of, and understand, his or her capabilities. One parent said, 'It is all about talking to your baby and recognising that when they are gurgling or smiling or making faces ... they are indicators of your child communicating with you.' (Barlow et al., 2007: 44)

> ## Focusing on early learning
>
> Other innovative programmes included focusing on early learning, including the sharing of books with babies during the first year of life. The PEEP programme (www.peep.org.uk) covers the period from the child's birth to starting school, and aims to promote parents' and carers' awareness of children's very early learning and development through making the most of everyday activities and interactions, to support parents/carers in their relationships with their children, and to enhance the children's self-esteem. During the weekly group sessions the leaders model different ways of sharing books with children, songs and rhymes are taught, and the contribution of everyday talk to children's development is emphasised.

Conclusion

In 2005 NESS (2005a) reported disappointing results in the outcomes that were measured, including parenting outcomes, though these were improved by 2008 (NESS, 2008). The results of this survey suggest that overall penetration of parenting support was low, and the quality of provision was insufficient to impact on parenting at a population level. Overall differences in outcomes between high- and low-performing programmes were small, but where they were observable they were consistent with the belief that areas providing good parenting support were achieving better parenting outcomes. These successful programmes were more likely to use nationally recognised standardised programmes, to use a manual, to give training to staff, to target their programmes on particular groups, to give written information to parents, and to focus on parenting and discipline. All this is consistent with the national and international literature on 'what works' in parenting and family support.

How can we explain the types of parenting support that emerged from Sure Start? Some responsibility lies with the vision formulated at the outset, particularly in the emphasis on bottom-up and 'needs-led' services, and the lack of firm direction about the type of support to be provided. This philosophy was used by a significant number of SSLPs to justify the development of programmes locally by staff who, though they had been doing this work for a lifetime, had no additional training or ongoing support.

The evidence base about 'what works' is fairly extensive, and although it supports a diverse range of programmes, the sort of changes that are wrought by such programmes are, on the whole, small. This suggests that the incoherent tapestry of often one-off interventions to support parenting that were being provided in the majority of SSLPs were not likely to make much impact on parenting at a population level.

References

Bakermans-Kranenburg, M.J., Juffer, F. and van IJzendoorn, M.H. (1998) 'Intervention with video feedback and attachment discussions: does type of maternal insecurity make a difference?', Infant Mental Health Journal, 19: 202–19.

Barlow, J., Kirkpatrick, S., Ball, M. and Stewart-Brown, S. (2007) Family and Parenting Support in Sure Start Local Programmes. Nottingham: DfES.

Barlow, J., Parsons, J. and Stewart-Brown, S. (2005) 'Systematic review of the effectiveness of group based parenting programmes for infants and toddlers', Child: Care, Health and Development, 31: 33–42.

Barlow, J. and Stewart-Brown, S. (2000) 'Review article: behavior problems and parent-training programs', Journal of Developmental and Behavioral Pediatrics, 21: 356–70.

Barnes, J. and Freude-Lagevardi, A. (2003) From Pregnancy to Early Childhood: Early Interventions to Enhance the Mental Health of Children and Families. London: Mental Health Foundation.

Belsky, J., Melhuish, E., Barnes, J., Leyland, A., Romaniuk, H. and the NESS Research Team (2006) 'Effects of Sure Start local programmes on children and families: early findings from a quasi-experimental, cross-sectional study', British Medical Journal, 332: 1476–8.

Bos, H., Huston, A.C., Granger, R., Duncan, G.J., Brock, T. and McLoyd, V.C. (1999) 'New hope for people with low incomes: two-year results of a program to reduce poverty and reform welfare.' San Francisco, CA: Manpower Demonstration Research Corporation in National Research Council and Institute of Medicine (2000) from Neurons to Neighbourhoods; The Science of Early Childhood Development. Washington, DC: National Academy Press.

Brooks-Gunn, J. and Duncan, G.J. (1997) 'The effects of poverty on children and youth', The Future of Children, 7(2): 55–71.

Conger, R.D., Conger, K., Elder, G., Lorenz, F., Simmons, R. and Whitbeck, L. (1992) 'A family process model of economic hardship and adjustment of early adolescent boys', Child Development, 63: 526–41.

Desforges, C. and Bouchaar, A. (2003) The Impact of Parental Involvement, Parental Support and Family Education on Pupil Achievement and Adjustment: A Literature Review, DfES Research Report 433. London: Department for Education and Skillls.

DoH (Department of Health) (2004) *Choosing Health: Making Healthier Choices Easier.* London: HMSO.

Dretzke, J., Frew, E., Davenport, C., Barlow, J., Stewart-Brown, S., Sandercock, J., Bayliss, S., Raftery, J., Hyde, C. and Taylor, R. (2005) 'The effectiveness and cost-effectiveness of parent training/education programmes for the treatment of conduct disorders, including oppositional defiant disorders, in children', *Health Technology Assessment*, 9(50): 1–250.

Egeland, B.E., Carlson, E. and Sroufe, A. (1993) 'Resilience as Process', *Development and Psychopathology*, 5: 517–28.

Farrington, D. (2003) *Early Prevention of Adult Antisocial Behaviour.* Cambridge: Cambridge University Press.

Melhuish, E.C., Belsky, J., Anning, A., Ball, M., Barnes, J., Romaniuk, H., Leyland, A. and NESS Research Team (2007) 'Variation in Sure Start local programme implementation and its consequences for children and families', *Journal of Child Psychology and Psychiatry and Allied Disciplines*, 48: 543–51.

Moran, P., Ghate, D. and Van der Merwe, A. (2004) *What Works in Parenting Support? A Review of the International Evidence.* London: HMSO.

Morris, P. and Michalopoulos, C. (2000) *The Self-sufficiency Project at 36 Months: Effects on Children of a Program that Increased Parental Employment and Income (Executive Summary).* New York: Social Research and Demonstration Corporation.

NESS (2005a) *Early Findings on the Impact of Sure Start Local Programmes on Child Development and Family Functioning: Final Report of the Cross-sectional Study of 9- and 36-month-old Children and Their Families*, Surestart Report 13. Nottingham: DfES. (Available at www.ness.bbk.ac.uk/documents/activities/impact/1183.pdf)

NESS (2005b) *Variation in Sure Start Local Programmes Effectiveness: Early Preliminary Findings*, Surestart Report 14. Nottingham: DfES. (Available at www.ness.bbk.ac.uk/documents/activities/impact/1184.pdf)

NESS (2008) The Impact of Sure Start Local Programmes on Three Year Olds and their Families. Nottingham: DfES (Available at www.ness.bbk.ac.uk)

Patterson, G.R., DeBaryshe, D. and Ramsey, E. (1989) 'A developmental perspective on antisocial behavior', *American Psychologist*, 44: 329–35.

Scaramella, L.V., Conger, R.D., Simons, R.L. and Whitbeck, L.B. (1998) 'Predicting a risk for pregnancy by late adolescence: a social contextual perspective', *Developmental Psychology*, 34: 1233–45.

Stewart-Brown, S. and Shaw, R. (2004) 'The roots of social capital: relationships in the home during childhood and health in later life', in A. Morgan and C. Swann (eds), *Social Capital for Health: Issues of Definition, Measurement and Links to Health.* London: Health Development Agency.

Tennant, R., Barlow, J., Goens, C. and Stewart-Brown, S. (2007) 'A systematic review of interventions to promote mental health and prevent mental illness in children and young people', *Journal of Public Mental Health*, 6(1): 25–32.

Zaslow, M.J., Pedersen, F.A., Suwalsky, J.T.D., Cain, R. and Fivel, M. (1985) 'The early resumption of employment by mothers: implications for parent–infant Interaction', *Journal of Applied Developmental Psychology*, 6: 1–16.

Suggested further reading

Barlow, J. and Stewart-Brown, S. (2000) 'Review article: behavior problems and parent-training programs', *Journal of Developmental and Behavioral Pediatrics*, 21: 356–70.

Barlow, J., Parsons, J. and Stewart-Brown, S. (2005) 'Systematic review of the effectiveness of group based parenting programmes for infants and toddlers', *Child: Care, Health and Development*, 31: 33–42.

Brooks-Gunn, J. and Duncan, G.J. (1997) 'The effects of poverty on children and youth', *The Future of Children*, 7(2): 55–71.

Moran, P., Ghate, D. and Van der Merwe, A. (2004) *What Works in Parenting Support? A Review of the International Evidence*. London: HMSO.

11 Domestic Abuse

Lisa Niven

This chapter:

- outlines versions of domestic abuse and examines its impact on families
- presents evidence of how Sure Start Local Programmes (SSLPs) addressed domestic abuse a) before disclosure, b) during abusive relationships and c) after disclosure
- discusses implications of lessons learned for children's centres.

Key questions:

- How would you define domestic abuse?
- What new opportunities did Sure Start offer for tackling domestic abuse?
- Why is a multi-agency approach essential both at the preventive and intervention stages?

Domestic abuse has been defined by the Department of Health as:

'Any incident of threatening behaviour, violence or abuse between adults who are or have been in a relationship together, or between family members, regardless of gender or sexuality.' (DoH, 2006)

One in four women and one in six men experience domestic abuse (United Nations, 2006; British Medical Association, 1998; Home Office, 1999). Of those women, 25 per cent are assaulted for the first time during pregnancy (Royal College of Midwives, 1997). Physical violence, which can be perpetuated over a period of time and may involve women as perpetrators, is a significant factor in many cases of domestic abuse. But it is accompanied by related forms of abuse: financial, emotional, psychological and sexual. Survivors say that it is psychological abuse – living in fear, being humiliated and bullied – that is the hardest thing to bear (Saunders and Humphreys, 2002).

If a woman is abused there is a high probability that her children will be abused (Radford et al., 2006). Around 750,000 children in the UK (DoH, 2005) are exposed to violence in the home and suffer effects as a result of witnessing, trying to intervene in abuse or of being dependent on an adult who is being abused. Children may be used as accessories in the abuse of a parent – as triggers of or a justification for violence. A woman with children may find it more difficult to leave a violent relationship.

It is more common to find domestic abuse in homes with young children (Brown and Bzostek, 2003). In 90 per cent of incidents, children are in the same or next room (Home Office, 1999). Children who witness domestic abuse are likely to have emotional and behavioural problems. Negative effects include poor health and sleeping habits and excessive crying (Jaffe et al., 1990). Infants and very young children exposed to domestic abuse experience distress which may affect brain development (Osofsky, 1999).

Developmental delay linked to the experience of domestic abuse can lead to poor educational performance, disrupted schooling, concentration difficulties and memory problems. Domestic abuse can also affect a child's social skills, since it can limit children's ability to feel empathy, increase aggressive behaviour and make them feel isolated and unable to make friends (Baldry, 2003; Fantuzzo and Mohr, 1999).

Once abused children have been made safe and secure, negative effects decrease. The mother's behaviour towards the children and her mental health are key factors in the recovery and resilience of children (Hughes and Luke, 1998). Children learn positive aspects of 'survivorship' when their mothers model assertive, but non-violent, responses to abuse (Peled, 1998).

Domestic abuse in SSLP areas

The extent of domestic abuse in SSLP areas was evident from data gathered through interviews with women who had children of 9 months and 3 years for the impact module of the National Evaluation of Sure Start. Of the 12,961 women who agreed to answer questions on domestic abuse, 5,803 said that they had experienced 'verbal aggression' at home while 1,858 said they had experienced 'domestic abuse'. There were no targets set by central government for SSLPs to address domestic abuse, but SSLP staff were aware of the prevalence of it in their communities and of its impact on families.

What SSLPs did to address domestic abuse

The themed study on domestic violence (Ball and Niven, 2007) explored evidence of good and innovative practice in addressing domestic abuse in 10 SSLP areas. Details of the methods used are in the report (www.ness.bbk.ac.uk/implementation.asp).

Three models of support for families were identified and will be discussed below:

- **before** any abuse had been experienced or disclosed: information provision and building trusting relationships;
- **during** an abusive relationship: managing crises, relocation for safety, working with families who chose to stay together;
- **after** disclosure: helping women come to terms with abuse, supporting them in remaining independent of their abuser, integrating them into the local community.

Before disclosure

Posters, leaflets and discreet cards small enough to be hidden in a purse, shoe or bra highlighting what constitutes domestic abuse and encouraging women to seek help by contacting local agencies were available in Sure Start buildings, usually displayed in women's toilets. The cards were taken by outreach staff to group sessions at other venues.

In areas of linguistic diversity SSLPs struggled to get their messages about domestic abuse across. Some SSLPs produced a single poster featuring a short message and contact details in a number of languages. Others used translators and family support workers. However, within small communities women were reluctant to disclose to workers who shared their cultures and beliefs because of fears over confidentiality. Despite these difficulties a home visitor reported that 'women in these communities are beginning to realise that abusive behaviour is not acceptable', but 'we are much further behind with the men who cannot see what the problem is'. Confidentiality was also a concern for workers from some communities. An SSLP with clients divided equally between white and Asian communities received no referrals from the Asian support workers working in the Asian community. The workers reported that they were unwilling to jeopardise their relationships with local families by being known to have helped women to leave their husbands, reported abuse and identified children at risk to social services.

Staff training related to domestic abuse varied. In some SSLPs all workers were trained in basic understanding of domestic abuse and awareness of diagnosing it. Staff training focused on instilling trust and being non-judgemental (but being honest about child protection duties) rather than on giving advice or persuading women to leave an abusive relationship. Other programmes trained key professionals, such as family support workers responsible for outreach work, community psychiatric nurses, childcare workers, midwives and health visitors. Others had a key worker with the responsibility for domestic abuse; for example, a parent involvement officer.

SSLP workers helped families access information and advice either by providing it directly or by facilitating access to specialist help. They offered crèche support and help with transport. It was important to forge links with other agencies. Often space within SSLP venues was provided for housing advice, Citizens' Advice Bureau, health workers and counselling services. For example, having received no referrals from the housing department, one SSLP invited them to attend partnership boards and offered room space for drop-in consultations with families. As a result, the manager reported that 'they understand now what we are looking out for and flag up families that could use our services'. For some women, knowledge provided by specialist agencies about the legal process and their right to advocacy, entitlement to benefits and help with debt, was the trigger for seeking help.

Most SSLPs reported that building relationships with women was the most effective means of detecting abuse. In one SSLP, a health visiting assistant regularly visited families where domestic abuse was suspected to maintain regular contact under the pretext of weighing the baby.

Good practice: avoiding dependency

The ultimate goal was to help those abused towards empowered independence by:

- being only one of a number of agencies involved;
- starting with a one-to-one relationship then moving women into groups;
- not making one family 'their own' but spreading responsibility beyond family support workers;
- providing regular supervision for staff so they could share responsibility for a family;
- training workers (in, for example, transactional analysis) to be aware of not keeping the abused person as 'victim'.

During disclosure

Sure Start staff recognised the building of a trusting relationship as the prerequisite for disclosure. Engaging women as early as the antenatal stage afforded time for a relationship to develop. Women tended to disclose to SSLP childcare workers because they saw them frequently as they dropped off their children in nurseries and crèches. Childcare workers were perceived as familiar, non-threatening and trustworthy. Staff were trained to listen for hints of abuse. As one manager told us, 'whatever women tell you, you can guarantee there's more that they haven't told'. Childcare workers knew *not* to give advice, but knew how to link clients with specialist advice and support, if necessary immediately. Referral between agencies was a strength of effective multi-agency teamwork. A health visitor said, 'We all know each other so we can signpost effectively'.

Women were afraid of the consequences of disclosure and often hinted at problems over a period of time: 'If I tell you something, will you tell anyone?' Waiting to establish trust and ensuring a family was not exposed to danger was a delicate balancing act. Discussions at group sessions about abuse prompted others to disclose. A family support worker reported, 'Women may come to a group and cracks appear, or they drop a phrase – usually this means they are ready to talk'.

SSLP practitioners witnessed family situations where children were affected by the abuse of their mother. Some mothers, afraid their son would grow up to act like their father, over-punished to compensate; children were puzzled about the explanation for the abuse and often blamed themselves; other children were told that the abuse was their fault. In one SSLP area the children in a family were encouraged by the abusive father to physically punish and restrain their mother whenever he was out of the house. Often recognition of the impact of abuse on their children prompted a parent to disclose.

Sometimes traditional values and beliefs within families and communities mitigated against tackling domestic abuse. A family support worker explained, 'We've had a couple of instances where gran has come as support for mum and has ended up also disclosing. "In our day it was natural, right?" But actually it has to do with the culture of a community'. A common perception is that the boundaries of abusive behaviour vary between cultures; but SSLPs reported abuse in a variety of family types, regardless of the ethnicity of the perpetrator or victim.

Families living with abuse tend to become isolated from family and friends and are unlikely to talk about their experiences. SSLPs depended on midwives and health visitors, who delivered universal home-based pre- and post-natal services, and who were alert to the signs of domestic abuse, to refer families at risk. The onus was on the programme to follow up referrals with phone calls and visits to assess need and formulate a care plan. In some SSLP areas midwives alerted the family to support and services available to them, but left them with the responsibility for action. A midwife reported, 'Ultimately it's up to the mum. 99 per cent of the time mum is sitting with the health visitor or midwife when she calls and can then speak to the link worker on the phone. Otherwise the mum has to contact the link worker herself'. Despite their best intentions to reach victims, SSLPs were aware that some were not identified through statutory health visits. Forging close links with housing officers could provide an alternative network for identifying families at risk.

Child protection issues do not arise in every case of domestic abuse, but it was SSLP policy to tell parents that if they disclosed something that put a child at risk, the programme was duty-bound to report it.

Good practice: a worker trained to be alert to reasons for a child's distress

A young woman approached a Sure Start worker because she was struggling with her son's behaviour. The support worker for teenage parents worked individually with the mother and child, who started attending a young mothers' group. Here the mother showed the worker a bruise on her child's arm, explaining that her partner became aggressive when he was drinking. The child was referred to Social Services, who offered new accommodation to the mother, which she turned down. A child protection conference was called, and a plan made. It was possible to talk openly with both parents about domestic abuse because the child was on the child protection register and because there was a care plan. The father was encouraged to reduce his drinking and undergo anger management. The mother was encouraged to use Sure Start services for herself and the child. The support worker continued to work with the mother to help her understand the connection between her son's behaviour and the violence at home. She suggested that the mother and father attended a parenting programme together.

Some women chose to remain in abusive relationships. One SSLP set up groups to support them. The family support worker responsible for the sessions explained:

'In these groups women talk about when they have defended children, taken a beating on their behalf. They don't want children taken away and think it's better to stay in the relationship and not create a fuss and risk losing the children. Victims will often make excuses for that [abusive] behaviour.'

Few SSLPs made contacts with male perpetrators of domestic abuse, although some referred men to anger management courses. A deputy programme manager's comment on their reluctance to involve men is typical: 'Work with fathers needs careful handling and coordinating when they come into the building as their partner or child may also be around.'

Men in SSLP areas were also subjected to domestic abuse. One SSLP employed a counsellor from Relate, seconded for two days a week, who gave his views on the differences between male and female abuse:

'We see lots of male victims. Generally speaking if women are the perpetrators, the violence is more premeditated, more systematic and clinical. This can be explained by size and strength. For a man, usually they can hit out and be physically violent on the spur of the moment, often after drinking. For women, it needs planning so they can be sure to have the upper hand. For example, the woman who got up early to get a knife and sat over her partner in bed holding the knife, so it was the first thing he saw when he woke up.'

Most SSLPs helped families create an escape plan in preparation for the day they were ready or compelled to leave: gathering important documents together and keeping them somewhere safe and secret, having a store of money, medicines, clothes and toys, and a list of important phone numbers. Some SSLPs were the first point of contact for women in crisis who wished to flee. One woman called her local SSLP saying she needed help to leave by 5 p.m. when her partner was due home from work, but did not want to go far. Because of links with the local homelessness unit, the programme arranged for the woman and her children to be housed temporarily in a B&B in the area. They were later re-housed further away for their safety. Another SSLP was about to close its doors one evening when a young woman with little English arrived asking for help. Because of the woman's immigration status and dependence on funding from the council's housing department, she was not able to stay at the local Asian woman's refuge. Instead she was taken by a bilingual support worker to another place of safety and supported in getting legal aid and access to her infant son.

After disclosure

For individual women, counselling, offered by Relate or a local provider, was a first step to understanding what was happening in their relationship and in gaining confidence to take action. Attendance at a group often followed. SSLPs offered two types of group with distinctive purposes:

- *Groups with open access aimed at survivors of domestic abuse*: Members shared insights into coping with and fleeing from abuse. A family support worker explained, 'They speak more freely because they are proud of having come out the other end'.
- *Groups aimed at clients who needed anonymity, often currently experiencing abuse*: A mother reported, 'We have rules about how we are with each other outside the group. When a woman first joins she is told that what is said in the group does not leave the group, unless it is a child protection issue. Then it would have to be passed on – that is made very clear. We also ask if she would like to be acknowledged outside the group. Some women are still in their relationship and don't want to be acknowledged on the street as it could be dangerous for them'.

Good practice: freedom programme

A small number of SSLPs offered a freedom programme, an intervention based around 12 themes. A member of the group explained, 'We are told at the end of one week what the theme will be the following week. It's very much about your feelings, your personal view on things'.

Other women commented:

'The reassurance I get from the group that it wasn't me … it's not your fault, you don't have to feel guilty, you are able to talk.'

'At the time I left, my children were on the At Risk register. I was given a support worker from Care Plus who told me about the group. It took a long time for me to pluck up the courage to go. I had no confidence. To a certain extent I didn't want to admit that it had been domestic violence, then I realised that there are other people in the same situation, I'm not the only one. I don't know why but this gave me more confidence.'

Some SSLPs included staff and families together in drama workshops or attended productions. A small number wrote and performed their own plays based on the group's experiences. The public staging and DVDs of these plays were used to raise awareness of domestic violence and abuse within communities.

Sure Start staff were likely to encounter distressing stories from families in crisis. Supervision was highlighted by all staff as an essential ingredient in enabling them to cope. A family support worker said:

'It's very important that we have supervision. When we see a mum we think is ready to leave but she doesn't or she returns, we can vent our frustration with our supervisor and not with the parent. It's a revelation to think, "I haven't failed, but I am a valuable partner in this long-term goal".'

The safety of staff, particularly those supporting families at home, was paramount. A family support worker reported, 'On one occasion I went to visit a house but got no reply. The father of this family had a high level of domestic violence and control. I could hear him telling everyone to be quiet'. Normal procedures were to leave details of staff whereabouts and the expected time of return at the centre.

SSLP services tended to focus on parents, raising awareness of the effects of abuse on young children and helping them to deal with behavioural problems. Services targeting abused children directly were rare. In one SSLP early years and parental involvement workers did creative work with children and older siblings focusing on respect, rather than domestic abuse alone, to try to break established cycles of abusive relationships.

Good practice: integration into a new community

One SSLP paid for workers from a Forest School,* including one male worker, to work with families from a local refuge for a day. The mothers were impressed, particularly with the male worker's interactions with their children. They felt he was a positive male role model. Listening to their feedback encouraged the refuge manager to invite the Forest School worker to run a crèche in the refuge. As he also worked as a learning assistant at the local school and at the family centre after-school club, families re-housed in this area from the local refuge felt that their children benefited from consistency in the children's relationship with the male worker.

*A Forest School is an area specially designed to give children access to recreation and play in a challenging outdoor environment. They are supervised by workers qualified in outdoor pursuits. Forest Schools are usually charitable organisations, or funded by local authorities.

There was little evidence of SSLPs working directly with local refuges for victims of domestic abuse, unless SSLP staff persisted in making regular contact with them. In these cases they helped women in refuges to fill in benefits forms, especially when they had fled their home without key documents, and to talk about useful local services. Support workers and parents also recognised that children temporarily housed in refuges needed help in their transition into a new community. But it was more common for refuges just to display leaflets for SSLP services or to provide safe spaces for meetings hosted by refuge workers.

Good practice: working with women's aid refuges

One SSLP ran a weekly arts and crafts group at a local refuge led by two family support workers, and supplied a crèche worker to take care of the children. The support workers found that the women tended to empathise and problem-solve together in this relaxed atmosphere. The refuge could be a hectic and anxious place, with families having to share bathroom and kitchen facilities with strangers. The women particularly appreciated this space and time away from their children to talk in an environment separate from the anxiety of everyday life in the refuge and to form friendships. One of the family support workers explained:

'We often found that women would get tired of being in the refuge and of having no familiar friends or family around and would start to talk of going back to their partner. The group was able to give positive encouragement.'

Re-housing a family fleeing abuse was often complicated, but in one SSLP area, tackling the problems as a team resulted in a change in local housing policy (see box below).

Good practice: effective links with housing

A mother with young children had a joint tenancy with an abusive partner. She left the home but her name remained on the tenancy agreement. The partner wrecked the place and left. She was liable for the damages and, because of the large unpaid bill in her name, was not eligible for re-housing. The SSLP negotiated with the estates manager on her behalf and as a result the bill was cleared and the woman re-housed. In this area the district policy changed. Cases were dealt with individually and one signature only was required for joint tenancies. Estates officers were made aware of the implications of domestic abuse and, if a woman agreed, would refer her to the SSLP, Social Services and the police.

Key messages

- Recent initiatives for tackling domestic abuse from central government include the National Domestic Violence Action Plan and the appointment of a national domestic abuse co-ordinator. The inititatives replicate good SSLP practice in identifying links between ante-and post-natal violence and depression in mothers.
- Progress has been made in breaking down barriers in communication and working practices between professionals, so that they work together to support families where there is domestic abuse.

- There is a continuing need to raise awareness of the impact of domestic abuse on children, with the public at large, and those who are experiencing abuse but who may be unaware of its effects.
- Some SSLPs addressed the needs of children at risk by developing innovative methods of informing and supporting communities around the dangers of domestic abuse and minimising risks from violent or abusive partners.
- All staff in contact with children and families should have a basic introduction to domestic abuse, be competent to recognise and query signs of abuse, and be familiar with government guidance on dealing with women and children who are abused.
- Early education and play services provide opportunities to model for children non-violent solutions and co-operative activities.

References

Baldry, A.C. (2003) 'Bullying in schools and exposure to domestic violence', *Child Abuse and Neglect*, 27(7): 713–32.

Ball, M. and Niven, L. (2007) *Domestic Violence and Sure Start Local Programmes.* Nottingham: DfES.

British Medical Association (1998) *Domestic Violence: A Health Care Issue?* London: BMA.

Brown, B.V. and Bzostek, S. (2003) 'Violence in the lives of children', *Cross Currents, Issue 1, Child Trends Data-Bank*, August.

DoH (Department of Health) (2005) *Domestic Violence: A Resource Manual for Health Care Professionals.* London: DoH.

DoH (Department of Health) (2006) *Working Together to Safeguard Children.* London: Stationery Office. (Available at www.everychildmatters.gov.uk/workingtogether/)

Fantuzzo, J. and Mohr, W. (1999) 'Prevalence and effects of child exposure to domestic violence', *The Future of Children* (Issue: Domestic Violence and Children), 9 (3) Winter: 21–32.

Home Office (1999) *Domestic Violence: Findings from a New British Crime Survey Self-completion Questionnaire.* London: HMSO.

Hughes, M. and Luke, D. (1998) 'Heterogeneity in adjustment among children of battered women', in G. Holden, R. Geffner and E. Jouriles (eds), *Children Exposed to Marital Violence*. Washington, DC: American Psychological Association.

Jaffe, P., Wolfe, D. and Wilson, S. (1990) *Children of Battered Women*. Newbury Park, CA: Sage.

Osofsky, J.D. (1999) 'The impact of violence on children', *The Future of Children* (Issue: Domestic Violence and Children): 9 (3), Winter: 33–49.

Peled, E. (1998) 'Parenting by men who abuse women: issues and dilemmas', *British Journal of Social Work*: 30: 25–36.

Radford, L., Blacklock, N. and Iwi, K. (2006) 'Domestic abuse with assessment and safety planning in child protection: assessing perpetrators', in C. Humphreys and N. Stanley, (eds), *Domestic Violence and Child Protection: Directions for Good Practice*. London: Jessica Kingsley.

Royal College of Midwives (1997) *Domestic Abuse in Pregnancy* (Position Paper No 19). Nottingham: RCM.

Saunders, H. and Humphreys, C. (eds) (2002) *Safe and Sound: A Resource Manual for Working with Children Who Have Experienced Domestic Violence*. Bristol: Women's Aid Federation of England.

United Nations (2006) *The United Nations Secretary-General's Study on Violence against Children*. Geneva: United Nations General Assembly.

Suggested further reading

Ball, M. and Niven, L. (2007) *Domestic Violence and Sure Start Local Programmes*. Nottingham: DfES.

DoH (Department of Health) (2006) *Working Together to Safeguard Children*. London: Stationery Office. (Available at www.everychildmatters.gov.uk/workingtogether/)

Humphreys, C., Hester, M., Hague, G., Mullender, A., Abrahams, H. and Lowe, P. (2000) *From Good Intentions to Good Practice: Working with Families where there is Domestic Violence*. Bristol: Policy Press.

Mullender, A., Burton, S., Hague, G., Imam, U., Kelly, L., Malos, E. and Regan, L. (2003) *Stop Hitting Mum!: Children Talk About Domestic Violence*. East Molesley: Young Voice.

Mullender, A., Hague, G., Imam, U., Kelly, L., Malos, E. and Regan, L. (2002) *Children's Perspectives on Domestic Violence*. London: Sage.

Useful websites

www.bristol.ac.uk/sps/research/fpcw/vawrg/default.shtml – the Violence Against Women Research group, based at Bristol University.

www.refuge.org.uk/ – information and advice for women, children and friends and family.

www.thehideout.org.uk – produced by Women's Aid, providing information and advice for children.

www.womensaid.org.uk/ – help for women and children and information on policy and campaigns.

www.womenandequalityunit.gov.uk – developing policies related to gender equality.

12 Building on Good Practice: Lessons for Children's Centres

Mog Ball and Angela Anning

Sure Start local programmes seemed like an answer in themselves: an innovative and exciting way to work for children and give them a great start. If they demonstrated anything, it was that 10 years was not going to be enough to realise that vision in the hard-pressed areas in which local programmes operated. In fact, they had been operational for only a much shorter time – around five or six years – when government announced a vastly extended programme of children's centres, which drew on the Sure Start local programme (SSLP) model.

Many of the principles which informed SSLPs persist in children's centres (DfES, 2006). They will eventually provide a universal offer of basic services to all families: information on day care availability and vacancies in the local area, advice on training, employment and job-seeking, and parenting skills development. Where families need more, centres will be expected to develop more extensive services, and in areas of disadvantage the full range is likely to look like an SSLP. But the study of the impact of SSLPs over their short life, carried out by the National Evaluation of Sure Start team, showed that the great start prophesied for young children was going to take a while to achieve (NESS, 2005a; NESS, 2008). The first findings from this study in 2005 showed significant but small changes in parental outcomes, such as higher levels of acceptance of children, less scolding and smacking, and better than expected home learning environments. These were welcome advances but they were only the beginning of effecting improvements. And there were no discernible outcomes in areas like child cognitive and language development, though indication of social gains gave some encouragement. The second findings in 2008 revealed a variety of beneficial effects for children and their families living in SSLP areas, when children were 3 years old.

What is most encouraging is that some programmes were making more difference than others, and as well as being effective in all they tried to do, these were also the best-run programmes (NESS, 2007). In these chapters there has been an investigation of the good practice of the best of SSLPs which, one hopes, will be transferred to children's centres. In this book we have focussed on what worked.

Reconfiguring the workforce

As children's centres are established across the country, there will be far more people working with children and families. Some of them will be in familiar jobs and professions, but others will be para-professionals and community volunteers, among them parents themselves. Working with volunteers and parents as colleagues will require professionals and practitioners to adapt their practice, and to recognise the enriching aspect of volunteers and parents working alongside them. But it brings with it the responsibilities of good management and sensitive deployment of these additional resources.

One of the successes of good SSLPs was the way they mobilised local people and provided them with opportunities to serve. Another was that they offered workers scope and freedom to work in new ways and with new colleagues.

Children's centres will offer these opportunities too, but with fewer resources and less autonomy, and will be run by local authorities. Sure Start began the process of mutual understanding between professions, a breaking down of boundaries and suspicions, a creation of shared language and a willingness to respect and learn from each other. It is to be hoped that this radical change can be sustained and the satisfaction that it offered workers will be continued as the reform of children's services is extended.

The new developments have implications for training the workforce for children's services. The reform strategy is responsible for establishing new ways of training for the new ways of working. The challenge will be not only to equip all those working with children with generic skills and knowledge, but also to train people as specialists. Once again a balance will be needed, and if reform is not orchestrated carefully by commissioners of training, local authorities and professional bodies, there may be resentment on the part of specialist staff, especially if it looks as though their pay and conditions of service will be changed.

New ways of working

Successful SSLPs demonstrated a core 'style', the essence of which was valuing people. Workers at all levels – from receptionist through to manager – treated people with respect, patience and without making judgements. They built on the strengths which children and adults brought to the programme, accentuating the positive and celebrating the central importance of children and family life. These were happy places to be, and the activities which were successful enabled parents to have a positive enjoyment of their role. This could motivate them to want to contribute to their own communities. Programmes could offer an opportunity to do so in enterprising ways – working in community cafés, creating community gardens, upgrading local parks and play facilities, running sports events, weekend treats and so on.

Reaching people

There is no doubt that for many families SSLPs delivered good experiences and were very popular. In particular, families where children had special needs were able to access tailored support quickly and with far less effort than they had been used to. This was because the capacity to help them was increased and because professional staff felt less worried about raising expectations they could not fulfil. Referrals to specialist services which had once meant families joining long waiting lists were now attended to quickly, so that they could receive immediate help and be signposted to a wider range of local resources. There were more services that could be delivered in the home, like speech and occupational therapy and Portage, there were more loan schemes for specialised equipment, there were more toy libraries and more help with transport. All this made a lot of difference and families were grateful for it.

But overall the reach figures for SSLPs were disappointing. Although most programmes achieved a high percentage (sometimes 100 per cent) of contacts with families with newborn babies (usually through midwife and health visitor services), reach figures for families with under-4s were rarely higher than 26 per cent. A further dilemma was that those who would have benefited most from Sure Start were the least likely to be reached. The evidence was that programmes built up core groups of users from families with young children who were mainly those who could attend services during school hours. This excluded many working parents and fathers. In addition, the tendency of regular users to appear to form dominating cliques could put off potential new users.

Workers appeared reluctant to persist in attempts to attract new users when they had already established a comfortably-sized clientèle. When asked why they were not reaching wider sections of the community, they tended to cite characteristics of the users rather than weaknesses in their own approach. For example, they attributed non-attendance by potential users to lack of confidence or apathy (NESS, 2007). It is not surprising that the impact study of NESS found that better-off families in SSLP areas gained most from the programme. The sort of families less likely to use services and benefit from them included lone single parents, very young parents, parents in workless households, and households with very low incomes (NESS, 2005a). Later findings (NESS, 2008) found less evidence that the most disadvantaged families and their 3 year olds were doing less well in SSLP areas. (for further details see NESS, 2008).

The message here is that persistence is needed to extend the reach of services to *all* sections of the community. This may mean that professionals will have to stretch themselves and think more creatively about the timing and nature of the services they offer, and the ways in which they do it. Outreach, the use of community venues and spaces which are sometimes defined as male territory, as well as intensive and regular home visiting by key workers well known to families, can all help increase reach and improve outcomes.

Reinforcing multi-agency links

The responsibility for children's services has shifted and is now located in new combined central government and local government departments which are dominated by the education agenda. The danger with this positioning is that other agencies, such as social work, health, housing and employment services, can be marginalised. NESS (2005b) demonstrated that where SSLPs were led by health authorities, or gave a strong role to those authorities, the outcomes for children were better. Health authorities could offer existing infra-structure, access to data-bases about families and had long expertise in working with families with children under 3 years. It is essential that PCTs and their staff are closely involved in the planning and delivery of services from children's centres. It will be up to managers of children's centres to ensure that this happens.

The benefit of the new, inclusive local children's service departments should be that all those working with children are seen as colleagues in a joint enterprise, working to common protocols and procedures, like the Common Assessment Framework. For example, a family support worker, whether employed by the social welfare system or the voluntary sector, should have a transparent and stronger relationship with their colleagues in education and health. If workers find that this is not happening, they will need to speak up and demand it.

Building on strong foundations

SSLPs have provided a foundation for good practice. They were themselves stronger and more effective where they built on an inheritance of good practice – local collaboration, high-quality early years and health services, and a strong commitment from the local authority. Building on strength is important – this process of taking the best from experience and moving forward will result in stable, consistent, well-staffed, well-resourced early years services. This must be the aspiration towards which we are all working, however long it takes.

The test of quality for early years services wherever they are offered must be: would you want them for your children? If those working in this field constantly test what they are doing against this criterion, we will create services of which we can be proud.

References

DfES (Department for Education and Skills) (2006) *Children's Centres Practice Guidance: November 2006*. London: DfES. (Available at www.SureStart.gov.uk)

NESS (2005a) *Early Findings of the Impact of the SSLPs on Child Development and Family Functioning: Final Report of the Cross-Sectional Study of the 9-month-old and 36-month-old Children and their Families*. Nottingham: DfES.

NESS (2005b) *Variation in SSLPs' Effectiveness: Early Preliminary Findings.* London: HMSO.

NESS (2007) *Understanding Variations in Effectiveness amongst Sure Start Local Programmes: Report 024.* Nottingham: DfES.

NESS (2008) The Impact of Sure Start Local Programmes on Three Year Olds and their Families. Nottingham: DfES.

Suggested further reading

Every Child Matters: Change for Children (2004)
(Available at www.everychildmatters.gov.uk)
United Nations Convention on the Rights of the Child (1990)
(Available at www. everychildmatters.gov.uk)

Index

Added to the page reference 'f' denotes figure, 'g' denotes glossary and 't' denotes table.